THE FOCAL EASY GUIDE TO
PREMIERE PRO

The Focal Easy Guide Series

Focal Easy Guides are the best choice to get you started with new software, whatever your level. Refreshingly simple, they do *not* attempt to cover everything, focusing solely on the essentials needed to get immediate results.

Ideal if you need to learn a new software package quickly, the Focal Easy Guides offer an effective, time-saving introduction to the key tools, not hundreds of pages of confusing reference material. The emphasis is on quickly getting to grips with the software in a practical and accessible way to achieve professional results.

Highly illustrated in color, explanations are short and to the point. Written by professionals in a user-friendly style, the guides assume some computer knowledge and an understanding of the general concepts in the area covered, ensuring they aren't patronizing!

Series editor: Rick Young (www.digitalproduction.net)

Director and Founding Member of the UK Final Cut User Group, Apple Solutions Expert and freelance television director/editor, Rick has worked for the BBC, Sky, ITN, CNBC and Reuters. Also a Final Cut Pro Consultant and author of the best-selling *The Easy Guide to Final Cut Pro.*

Titles in the series:

The Easy Guide to Final Cut Pro 3, Rick Young

The Focal Easy Guide to Final Cut Pro 4, Rick Young

The Focal Easy Guide to Final Cut Express, Rick Young

The Focal Easy Guide to Maya 5, Jason Patnode

The Focal Easy Guide to Discreet Combustion 3, Gary Davis

The Focal Easy Guide to Premiere Pro, Tim Kolb

THE FOCAL EASY GUIDE TO
PREMIERE PRO

For New Users and Professionals

TIM KOLB

International Academy of
Design & Technology
39 John Street
Toronto, Ontario M5V 3G6

AMSTERDAM • BOSTON • HEIDELBERG • LONDON
NEW YORK • OXFORD • PARIS • SAN DIEGO
SAN FRANCISCO • SINGAPORE • SYDNEY • TOKYO

Focal Press is an imprint of Elsevier

Focal Press is an imprint of Elsevier
200 Wheeler Road, Burlington, MA 01803, USA
Linacre House, Jordan Hill, Oxford OX2 8DP, UK

Library of Congress Cataloging-in-Publication Data
Application submitted.

British Library Cataloguing-in-Publication Data
A catalogue record for this book is available from the British Library.

ISBN: 0-2408-0567-4

For information on all Focal Press publications visit our website at
www.focalpress.com

04 05 06 07 08 10 9 8 7 6 5 4 3 2 1

Typeset by Kolam Information Services Pvt. Ltd, Pondicherry, India
Printed in Italy

Dedication:

To Marianne, Samantha and Cameron,

because it's Husband/Father, Producer/Director

...in order of importance.

Contents

Editing 63

Effects 93

Foreword

My first exposure to Adobe Premiere dates back to the introduction of QuickTime. I'm embarrassed to admit that I was so tied up in the video production equipment we were using then that I really questioned the significance of this little novelty portion of the Apple Macintosh OS to professionals, as I watched some small, low-resolution, low–frame rate video that my partner had captured off the television to demonstrate the wonders of his brand-new Macintosh Quadra 840.

In those early days, Adobe Premiere was one of very few players in nonlinear video editing. My next recollection of Adobe Premiere was of versions 3.0 and 4.0, when a gentleman named Flavio Kampah was exploring what could be done with motion graphics, just before we went to nonlinear editing in our own facility in the mid-'90s.

But that was then.

These days, I do my video editing, compositing, audio posting, graphics, encoding, and authoring (media and print) on desktop computers—much of it on the laptop I'm typing on right at this moment. Adobe Premiere Pro is my pivotal tool in video post-production.

In many ways, Adobe Premiere Pro is a software program that has come of age. Users of past versions of Adobe Premiere, like me, will find the layout and some of the philosophy a bit different from the Premiere of the past. However, once you've learned about its features and toolset, I suspect you will never want to go back. New users will find a powerful video editor with completely new audio capabilities, in addition to more real-time functionality than many editing applications that cost considerably more.

Premiere Pro can truly take its place alongside Photoshop, Illustrator, and After Effects as a professional tool of the same pedigree. Professionals and enthusiasts alike will appreciate what the latest version of Adobe's long-time video editor has to offer.

Before we go any further, I need to mention David Kuspa, technical editor of *The Easy Guide to Premiere Pro*. His contributions were invaluable and focused, and there is no doubt this is a superior publication because of him. I am grateful for his insight.

Our goal is that this book gets you up to speed with Premiere Pro in short order, giving you the tools you need to be successful with the software very quickly. I suppose a good place to start that philosophy would be to wrap up this introduction and get to it.

So be it.

Tim Kolb
Producer/Director

SET UP

Setting up the Hardware

To use Adobe Premiere Pro, you will need a computer with Microsoft Windows XP or Windows XP Pro operating system. The minimum processor and configuration necessary is an Intel Pentium III 800 MHz or an AMD Athlon MP or XP. In order to run Adobe Premiere Pro comfortably, however, you will need a computer outfitted with a relatively fast Pentium 4. Adobe recommends a 3.0 GHz processor. Adobe Premiere Pro is designed to make excellent use of hyperthreading CPUs.

You will also need a way to capture video and audio to, and output video and audio from, your computer. Many of us use a basic FireWire card with our DV equipment; others may use add-on boards or even software plug-ins that can handle many types of analog and digital video, standard definition, high definition, etc.

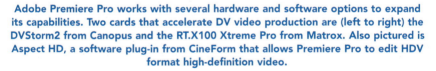

Adobe Premiere Pro works with several hardware and software options to expand its capabilities. Two cards that accelerate DV video production are (left to right) the DVStorm2 from Canopus and the RT.X100 Xtreme Pro from Matrox. Also pictured is Aspect HD, a software plug-in from CineForm that allows Premiere Pro to edit HDV format high-definition video.

The procedures and behaviors of each of these boards are different, and covering every possibility is beyond the scope of this book. We will cover setup for a basic FireWire card (also referred to as an *IEEE-1394 card* or an *iLink interface*) and will assume this configuration when referring to hardware. If you use a third-party video capture/output card with Adobe Premiere Pro, please refer to the documents that came with your video card for setup instruction.

When setting up your system, in the case of DV video and FireWire, there are several things to keep in mind.

There are two types of FireWire connectors: one is usually referred to as a *six-pin* and the other as a *four-pin*. The six-pin connector is the one most likely to exist on your computer and on any external FireWire hard drives you may use. The smaller, four-pin connector would most likely be seen on videotape decks and camcorders.

The two can be mixed in a system where you need to hook up both, but the correct cables must be used (six to six-pin, four to four-pin, and a six to four-pin).

If you are using DV video in your production and your computer has only one hard drive (the C drive), I would recommend that you get additional hard drives for video and audio. IDE hard drives continue to come down significantly in price and are more than fast enough for DV's relatively low data rate. External FireWire hard drives are a slightly more expensive option for cases in which you might need to transport large amounts of data from machine to machine or are working on a laptop, but they aren't as fast as IDE drives mounted internally in a desktop machine. An 8 MB buffer is recommended for the best performance with the fewest playback hiccups.

IDE drives should be fast enough for most uses, possibly including even uncompressed video. Other types of drive arrangements may be recommended by some companies that manufacture third-party cards, for performance reasons. For most purposes, however, the more expensive SCSI hard drives and multiple-drive RAID configurations are becoming far less necessary than they once were.

I would also recommend that you set up your system to include an NTSC or PAL video monitor to view your work. This can be done by converting the FireWire out to an analog video signal through a camcorder or VCR by outputting FireWire to the device and taking analog video and audio out to the video monitor. This can also be done with a variety of specialized converters that are available to convert FireWire to analog video and audio, minimizing wear on your camcorder. Using a video monitor will give you a better idea of how your finished video will actually look on a television, as opposed to how it may look on your computer monitor.

Loading the Software

Loading Adobe Premiere Pro on your Windows XP or Windows XP Pro computer system is as easy as inserting the CD-ROM and following the prompts. One difference that many current users may notice is that Apple's QuickTime is no longer installed with Premiere Pro. Premiere Pro is capable of working with QuickTime files, but you will have to install the latest version of QuickTime on your system yourself if you don't already have it.

Premiere Pro's install CD dialogue.

Project Setup

When you launch Premiere Pro, you will be asked to choose between creating a new project or opening an existing project. Once you've been working with Premiere Pro for a while, a list of recently saved projects will appear in the upper part of the dialogue as a convenience.

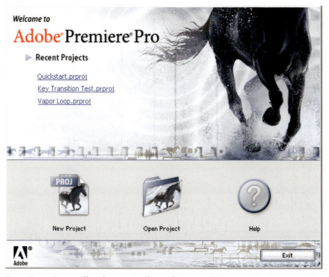

**Premiere Pro will ask you to launch an existing project or create
one. "Untitled" projects are a thing of the past.**

If you choose to start a new project, you will find yourself in the New Project
dialogue. Most of us will use a common preset for our work. The presets are listed
on the left, and they cover most common formats in NTSC and PAL standards.

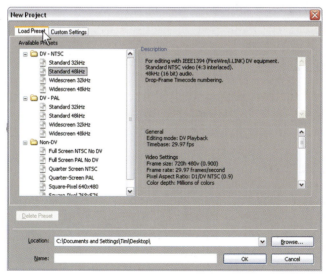

New Project window.

If you have a hardware card or specialized software plug-in installed that has a specific Project Preset of its own, you should see that setting listed among the standard presets. (Check the documentation that came with your third-party software or hardware for details.) The system being pictured in this instance is using the standard DV NTSC project presets.

If none of the standard presets meets your needs, you can create a custom preset by clicking on the Custom Settings tab on the top left of the window. From here, you can access frame size, video codec (COmpressor/DECompressor), pixel aspect ratio, and other technical setup parameters for your project. Make sure you familiarize yourself with the necessary specifications for your project before you make adjustments in the Custom Settings window.

Past users of Premiere will notice that you can no longer change your project settings in the course of working on a project. This is to increase speed and minimize configuration conflicts.

The general settings panel in the New Project Custom Settings window.

A couple of the settings are worth noting in these dialogues. They don't necessarily have much to do with the technical video processing setup, but with your preferred ways of working. Check the following settings:

Under General:

- The Title Safe and Action Safe window sizes are adjustable here if you find it necessary. Make sure to check both dimensions.

- The Playback Settings button will take you to the Settings dialogue, which allows you to set how the video and audio you are editing will play back. If you have external hardware or sound cards that you wish to use for playback, or if you want to gain speed and increase real-time playback on your system by disabling some playback options, this is where you do it.

Click on the Playback Settings button to set up real-time video and audio playback.

Under Capture:

- You can choose what video capture device you want to use if you have more than one. The default for most of us using DV will be DV/IEEE 1394 Capture (FireWire card).

Choose your capture card.

Under Video Rendering:

- Compressor and Color Depth are accessible from here if your Project Preset supports options.

- Optimize Stills can help you save data space and rendering time by processing a still frame held for a period of time on the timeline as a still frame "frozen," instead of handling it like a video clip. The default for this is checked.

Under Video Rendering, the compressor and color depth may not be adjustable if the Project Preset doesn't support multiple codecs.

Set up the track structure of your default project, designating the number and type of tracks.

Under Default Sequence:

- All these settings determine what your New Project will look like when you create one. Number of video tracks and type and number of audio tracks can be specified here

so that you start with a sequence in the Timeline window that makes the most sense to you. Audio tracks are specific, so you will want to create the type of audio tracks you will use. Stereo clips can't be placed on a mono track, mono clips can't be placed on a 5.1 track, etc.

Your saved custom Project Preset will be available under Available Presets.

If the settings you have chosen in the Custom Settings dialogue are going to be a common setup for you, you can choose to save your settings with the Save Preset button at the bottom of the window. The name you give the preset when you save it will be available to you the next time as a profile in the Settings menu with the standard presets, selectable with a single click.

Once you have set up the Project Settings, you will need to specify what the project will be called and where you will save it. How you store and organize your files is up to you, and optimal methods may be different, depending on your circumstances. In general, keeping a project and its associated files (video, audio, graphics, etc.) in order will always pay off later.

Some recommendations:

1 Keep your Premiere Pro Project files on a separate hard drive from your C drive, and keep your conformed audio files on a separate drive from your video and audio files, if possible.

2 Video or audio files should be kept off the C drive or system drive of your computer. It will help your system to run more efficiently.

3 Rule #2 becomes even more important if you use a laptop. Even though the internal laptop drives are getting faster, there are still many that spin at 4200 rpms. Even in the case of DV, which is a relatively small datastream, this will almost certainly not be fast enough for even basic real-time playback.

Preferences

Once you've launched the program, you'll need to set up the preferences. From the pulldown menu, select Edit ▶ Preferences.

General

In/out points show media offset:

This option allows you to choose whether Premiere Pro shows timcode for each clip as starting at zero or shows the timecode from the source tape.

The General heading in Edit ▶ Preferences.

Preroll and Postroll

This setting controls the preroll and postroll of

your video device during capture. For most DV devices, 2 to 5 seconds should be fine. You may want to adjust to your specific equipment if necessary.

Video Transition Default Duration

This setting controls the starting duration of all your transitions when you first place them on the timeline. The default is set to 30 frames, or 1 second. I typically run mine at 10 frames, as I find myself usually using significantly less than a second for most dissolves—which make up 99% of the transitions I do in my daily work.

Audio Transition Default Duration

This setting controls the starting duration of your audio transitions. The default is 0.5 seconds.

User Interface Brightness

Slide the slider to lighten or darken the screen interface. Where you like this best will probably be somewhat dependent on room lighting.

Audio

Automatch Time

Set this to affect the time the slider takes to return to its previous position when using Touch record mode in the audio mixer. (More on this on page 142.)

5.1 Mixdown Type

> Use this to set up the way Premiere Pro will mix down the six
> channels of surround sound to stereo for mastering to video
> devices or file types that don't support surround sound. Left/right
> channel assignments can get a little muddy if you include the low
> frequency effects (LFE) channel in the mixdown. You may want
> to experiment with whether or not you want to include it in the
> mixdown.

Play Audio While Scrubbing

> You have the option not to hear the audio on the timeline while
> you're moving the CTI back and forth on the timeline. I prefer to
> leave this checked, but if your system is hesitant when you are
> scrubbing the timeline, you may want to uncheck this box to
> improve performance.

Audio Hardware

You should see
your audio card in
the Input/Output
Device pop-up
menu. Be sure it
is selected. Below
that is the Output
Channel Mappings
control, where
each surround
sound channel is
sent during
playback on a
stereo sound
card.

Auto Save

You can have the box checked to save projects automatically as you work. Under the check box, set the time increment between automatic saves and the maximum number of project versions Premiere Pro keeps in archive. These files can be found in the folder *[current user]*/My Documents/Adobe/Premiere Pro/7.0/Project-Archive.

Capture

Select the check boxes to Abort capture when a dropped frame is detected and to Report any dropped frames. You can also elect to have Premiere Pro create a batch log if a batch capture doesn't finish successfully.

Device Control

Pick the proper device control from the pop-up. If you are using a DV device, options for model and manufacturer of each device can be accessed with the Options button. Preroll controls how far a video device backs up to get up to speed before capturing a section of video. Timecode Offset compensates for slight errors some equipment may cause by a slight delay between reaching a timecode point and actually starting or stopping a capture or an export to tape.

Label Colors

You can use color labels to help organize your media. This area of Preferences allows you to customize these colors.

Label Defaults

You can make certain colors the assigned color for certain types of media in the Project window and on the timeline.

Scratch Disks

Set the scratch disks to target where certain media gets saved on your system.

Captured Video and Captured Audio are the settings for where the media you capture from your video device are stored.

Video and Audio Previews are the files created when you render a sequence.

Conformed Audio is audio material that Premiere Pro creates in an uncompressed format to speed editing. Adobe recommends that this go to a different drive from the rest of your video and audio, if possible.

Still Images

Set the Default Duration for a still image when it loads. The default is 30 frames.

Preferences

General	Still Images
Audio	
Audio Hardware	Default Duration: 30 frames
Auto Save	
Capture	
Device Control	
Label Colors	
Label Defaults	
Scratch Disks	
Still Images	
Titler	
Trim	

OK   Cancel   Help

Titler

These preferences are for setting how the style swatches and the font browser show you your options. After we have discussed the Title Designer in more detail, you may want to customize these displays.

Preferences

General	Titler
Audio	
Audio Hardware	Style Swatches: Aa (2 characters)
Auto Save	Font Browser: AaegZz (6 characters)
Capture	
Device Control	
Label Colors	
Label Defaults	
Scratch Disks	
Still Images	
Titler	
Trim	

OK   Cancel   Help

Trim

You can set the Large Trim Offset for use in the Trim window. We will cover the Trim window in more detail. Leave this setting at the default values until you have used the Trim window and determined whether you would like to change these settings.

THE INTERFACE

Introduction to the Interface

The interface for Adobe Premiere Pro is made up of different work areas, each inside its own window. A two-monitor computer desktop is handy, though not required. Premiere Pro has many windows, and without two monitors, you may find yourself juggling windows a bit. Using the preset workspaces, as well as developing your own, can help you make the most efficient use of screen space.

Personally, I have a hectic travel schedule, and I use a laptop to do much of my postproduction work. I use Premiere Pro on its single screen quite often with no issues. For the purposes of this book, we will work with single-screen workspaces.

One bit of important information: There are *windows* and there are *palettes* in the Premiere Pro interface. The Tool, History, and Info palettes stay in front of everything so that they can be easily accessed. Windows can be brought to the front or back, like most software windows. Try to keep your palettes off to the side a bit, or you will constantly be moving them out of the way when you're trying to do other things.

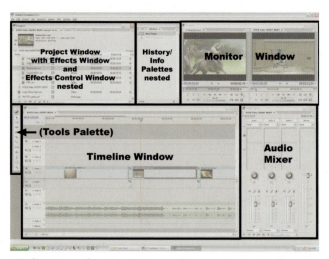

My laptop workspace. I've opened every window to show an overview. It isn't always practical or efficient to work with this many windows open.

Project Window

The Project window is where the elements of your project are stored. Video, audio, or graphics clips, titles, and sequences can be organized in separate folders

The Project window.

called *bins*. The Project window can be searched for media using specific criteria and can be used to visually preorder, or *storyboard*, clips for rough layout purposes.

The Monitor Window

The Monitor window contains the Source Monitor and the Program Monitor.

The Monitor window.

The Program Monitor, on the right side, shows the video from the sequence open in the Timeline window. As you scrub or play back from your Timeline window, the Program Monitor will show you the video that corresponds to the position of the CTI, or *current time indicator*. The CTI is the large sliding "cursor" in the Timeline window. Multiple Sequences will be available from tabs in both the Timeline window and the Program Monitor.

The Source Monitor lets you preview your source material and trim a clip before laying it on the timeline.

Each monitor pane can be assigned a display mode from the wing menu. Test displays are available here, as well as image quality adjustment to scale performance to your system.

Monitor window with wing menu.

The Timeline Window

The Timeline window contains your edited sequences. Each sequence is a self-contained edit "timeline" in itself. Multiple sequences are useful for creating multiple versions of your program, or as submaster sequences, where each segment of your program can be worked on separately and multiple sequences assembled in a final master sequence.

The Timeline window.

The Effects Window

The Effects window contains four folders:

- Audio Effects

- Audio Transitions

- Video Effects

- Video Transitions

The Effects window.

Use the effects and transitions in these folders by opening the appropriate folder and dragging the filter or transition to the timeline. The filters are typically dropped on a clip; the transitions must be dropped on an edit point, or the in or out point of a clip.

The Effect Controls Window

The Effect Controls window is where you will customize the settings for each filter or transition. The intrinsic or Fixed Effects controls—opacity, motion,

The Effect Controls window.

and audio volume—are easily accessed from here. Attributes for nearly anything can be fully keyframed for each clip and filter from this window.

The Audio Mixer Window

The Audio Mixer window is where adjustments can be made to the audio track volume, and effects can be added to each audio track. Premiere Pro can use mono, stereo, and channel surround sound audio tracks in the same project, and each track will have a channel on the audio mixer. Each track will accept files of the designated type. Stereo clips will only go to a stereo track, mono to a mono track, etc.

There are several configurations that you can use. The Audio Mixer is a large window when it is completely open, so it can take up valuable space on a single-monitor system. There are three basic choices for displaying the Audio Mixer:

1 When fully open, the Audio Mixer can display the Effects/Sends section in the top half of the window.

2 The Effects/Sends area can be hidden, leaving only the VU meters and volume controls, by clicking on the triangle to the left of the automation options.

3 To minimize the space taken up by the Audio Mixer window, yet maintain a view of

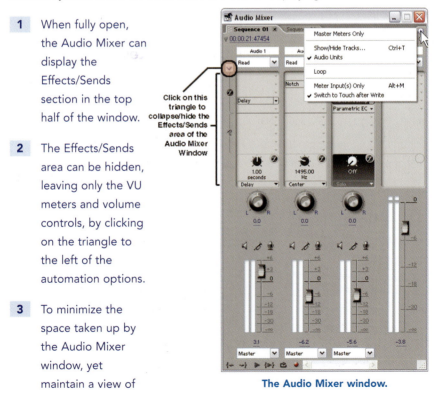

Click on this triangle to collapse/hide the Effects/Sends area of the Audio Mixer Window

The Audio Mixer window.

the master VU meters, select Master Meters Only from the wing menu. Master meters can be helpful for continuous monitoring of the overall audio level, without consuming as much screen space as the Audio Mixer.

The Tool Palette

The Tool palette contains the various tools that change the cursor's function to accomplish the many tasks necessary to edit video and audio. The Tool palette can be oriented vertically or horizontally by right-clicking outside of a tool button (but inside the window) and choosing Arrange Vertical or Arrange Horizontal from the context menu. Because the horse is just there to remind us of the logo, I like to use the horse as an easy area to click on to make this change.

Tabbed Windows and Palettes

Some Premiere Pro windows contain *tabs*, which look like small file folder tabs in the upper part of the window, starting on the left. Many of these windows can be combined, or *docked*, within one workspace window. To combine two or more windows as tabbed combinations, simply drag one window (by clicking and dragging the tab portion of the window) into another window.

The Tool palette.

Tabs can't be randomly combined. Here are the possible combinations:

1 The Monitor, Timeline, and Audio Mixer windows contain tabs for multiple sequences. Clicking a tab activates that tab's sequence in all three windows. The Timeline tabs representing multiple sequences can be dragged away to form separate timeline windows for each sequence.

2   The Effect Controls window can be docked in the Source view of the Monitor window, or it can be docked in the Project and Effects windows. I prefer it in the Project window, myself, because it gives me more room to work than the Source Monitor does.

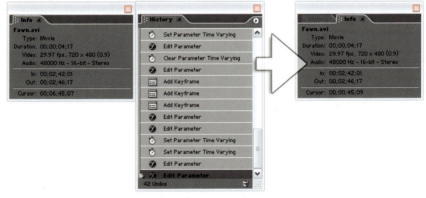

The Effects and Effect Controls windows can be docked inside the Project window to conserve workspace.

3   The History palette works like the Photoshop History tab. It keeps a list of your commands and can be used to step back to an earlier stage of your project if you need to undo a considerable amount of work. It can be combined with the Info palette.

The Info and History palettes.

4 The Info palette shows information that changes as you work, such as clip duration, timeline position, and start and end timecodes for the clip you have selected.

History   **Info** ✕

Fawn.avi
Type: Movie
Duration: 00;00;04;17
Video: 29.97 fps, 720 × 480 (0.9)
Audio: 48000 Hz – 16-bit – Stereo

In: 00;02;42;01
Out: 00;02;46;17

Cursor: 00;00;45;09

The Info palette.

If the Premiere Pro window isn't wide enough to display all tabs inside a docked window, there will be a slider above the tabs to scroll the tabs left or right so you can access them.

Use the slider above the tabs to scroll to a tab that is hidden due to a narrow window.

Arranging the Workspace

The workspace is completely adjustable, and you can move and size windows to your own preferences.

There are several default workspace choices in the Window ▶ Workspace ▶ pulldown menu.

Premiere Pro default workspace layouts.

These workspaces—for Editing, Color Correction, Audio Mixing, and Effects—are optimized to those functions. The windows you will need are organized efficiently, and the ones you are less likely to need are closed and not taking up valuable screen space.

You can change workspaces through the course of editing your project because rearranging your workspace strictly reorganizes your desktop display and does not affect your content.

Creating a Custom Workspace

Many users find they prefer a custom workspace layout to suit their own needs. You can adjust the windows and palettes in an arrangement that makes sense to you. Choose Window ▶ Workspace ▶ Save Workspace to save the setting. Your custom setting will now be in the list with the default settings in the Window ▶ Workspace menu.

As in the case of the default settings, you may want to consider creating workspaces for each major step in the editing process to maximize efficiency for each task.

Title	Window	Help		
	Workspace ▶	Tims Workspace		
		Tims PPro		
	Effects			
	Effect Controls	Editing	Shift+F9	
		Effects	Shift+F10	
	History	Audio	Shift+F11	
	Info	Color Correction	Shift+F12	
	Tools			
		Save Workspace.		
	Audio Mixer	Delete Workspace.		
	Monitor			
	Project			
	Timelines ▶			

Name and save your custom workspace.

For instance, when you are working on effects, you need the Effect Controls window to be accessible and large enough to work with. On the other hand, you may not need the Effect Controls window at all during the audio mixing phase of your edit.

Creating separate workspaces for each of these steps can streamline your workflow and make the process easier on your eyes, using larger windows when you need them the most. Look at each default workspace as a starting point, and customize from there.

CAPTURING MEDIA IN PREMIERE PRO

Premiere Pro brings media into a project in two ways: capturing and importing. *Capturing* refers to transferring video and/or audio to your hard drive from a video device, such as a camcorder, and making that file available to the project in the Project window. *Importing* is when a file already exists on your hard drive and you simply want to make it available to your project through a link in the Project window.

Opening the Capture Window

Press F5 or select Capture from the File pulldown menu. The Capture dialogue will open. In the upper right corner of the screen, you will see two tabs: one labeled Logging and one labeled Settings.

The Capture window. As you can see, the first thing I need to do is change the destination settings so I don't put media on my C drive.

The first order of business is just where your video and audio data will go when you capture it. It is recommended you keep your video and audio media on a hard drive other than your C or system drive. To specify a destination for your media, select the Settings tab. On the right side of the window, you will notice an area labeled Capture Locations about halfway down the window. You can specify locations on your system's hard drives for both the audio and the video. Again, be sure to target your media to drives other than your C drive. The remaining free space on your chosen hard drive will be displayed here. It can be helpful to have some idea of just how much space you may need. With DV, for instance, the rule of thumb is about 1 GB of hard drive space for every 5 minutes of video.

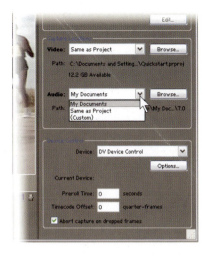

The Logging tab is where you log the in and out points of clips on your tape and create a *batch list* of predesignated clips for Premiere Pro to access and capture in a single step.

Capturing your video and audio with Premiere Pro can be done in one of three ways:

1 You can capture it on the fly by manually starting and stopping the capture process as your tape plays.

2 You can set an in point and an out point for a section you wish to capture.

3 You can set in and out points for a group of clips that you wish to capture as a batch.

Setting up Deck Control

Premiere Pro will control DV devices via the familiar video playback, or transport, controls in the Capture window, provided you have a FireWire card (IEEE-1394) installed in your computer. Premiere Pro will control other types of video devices with third-party controller software. If you have a third-party deck controller, please check your documentation for instructions.

The device transport controls (Play, Stop, Fast Forward, Rewind, etc.) are below the video screen in the Capture window. However, most editors find it infinitely more efficient to use keyboard shortcuts during capture and most frequently performed editing tasks.

The keyboard shortcuts (shown in the figure for clarity) are used throughout Premiere Pro (and many other video-editing software packages), so they are worth learning.

To set up Adobe Premiere Pro for software DV deck control, follow these steps:

Key	Function
J (repeat)	Shuttle reverse
J	Play in reverse
K	Stop
L	Play forward
L (repeat)	Shuttle forward
I	Set in point
O	Set out point
Spacebar	Toggle Play/Stop

1   Open the Capture window, click on the tab in the upper right-hand corner of the window, labeled Settings.

2   In the text field labeled Device, be sure that DV Device Control, or the appropriate device control for your system, is selected. (The first time you launch, it may default to None.)

3   In the lower part of the tab, you will see an area labeled Device Control. Click the Options button.

4   A window will open, allowing you choose the video standard, as well as the brand and type (model) of your video deck or camcorder. Choose the appropriate settings.

5   Check the indication for device status, making sure it says Online.

Once your device is connected, you can begin capturing footage. There are several different methods for capturing.

Manual Capture

To capture your video "on the fly," you can press the Play button in the Capture window or press the spacebar or the L key to put your video deck or camcorder into play mode. If you don't have a system with deck control, you can also operate your video device directly by pressing Play, Fast Forward, etc. Click the red Record button in the bottom of the window or press the G key to start capturing video. You can stop the capture by pressing Escape.

The Record button for manual capture in the bottom of the Capture window.

Capture In to Out Point

You can capture a clip beginning and ending at the points you set by doing the following:

1 Use the Play and Rewind/Fast Forward buttons or, on your keyboard, the J (reverse shuttle), K (stop), and L (play/shuttle forward) keys to position your tape at the point you wish to begin capturing. Press the button marked Set In to mark the point.

2 Go to the end of the section you wish to capture by playing or fast-forwarding to the point where you want the clip to end. When you reach the end point, mark it by selecting Set Out. You will notice that Premiere Pro displays the duration of your clip just below the in and out points.

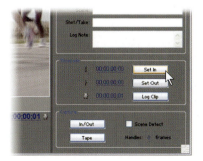

3 By clicking on the button marked In/Out, you will see Premiere back the tape up and capture the clip between the in and out points that you have set.

4 Name the clip or confirm the name you assigned it in the Capture window at the end of the capture.

Batch Capture

If you follow the first two steps in the Capture In to Out Point section and replace the third step with clicking on Log Clip, the clips will accumulate in the Project window but will remain offline, or uncaptured, until you elect to capture them all as a group. *Batch capturing* is a convenient way to capture many predesignated clips by timecode while you take a break or do something else.

Here's how to capture the clips you have logged:

1 Select all the clips in the Project window you wish to capture by Control-clicking or Shift-clicking on the clips. They will darken to indicate they are selected.

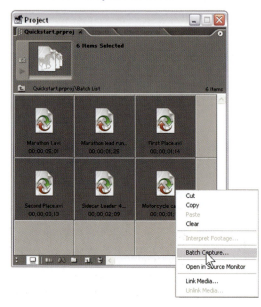

2 After you've selected the group of clips, right-click on any of the clips to bring up a context menu.

3 From the menu, choose Batch Capture.

4 Your video deck or camcorder may ask you to confirm that the proper reel or tape is in the deck. After you've confirmed that it is, the deck will begin to capture—and you can grab a cup of coffee.

Important note: Particularly in the case of some "prosumer" decks and camcorders, some timecode problems may present themselves if there is a break in the timecode. It's important to have continuous timecode so that the batch capture can work correctly.

Many consumer and so-called prosumer cameras can create a timecode break if several recordings are made on a blank tape. Unfortunately, most DV cameras will default back to 00:00:00:00 timecode at those breaks, making continuous capture or batch capture impossible, because the timecode repeats itself.

The best way to avoid this is to "black" your tapes before using them. Put the new video cassette in your camcorder and record the entire tape with the lens cap on. This will create continuous timecode on your tape, even if the camcorder ends up recording with gaps.

Automatic Scene Detection

There are times when it can be an advantage to capture an entire tape at once, but very inconvenient to work with one file that large. *Automatic scene detection* can be used to capture a tape and break the shots apart at detected recording start and stop points. It does this primarily by detecting breaks in the time stamp on the source tape.

There is an important distinction to be made here between time stamp and timecode. The *time stamp* is strictly a clock signature your camera is recording with the video. When you pause the tape for a period of time, that time stamp is discontinuous at that point. In contrast, *timecode* is the numbering system for each frame on your tape.

The Scene Detect button is below the video picture in the Capture window and, alternately, there is a checkbox in the lower right. Remember to turn it off if you're not using it. It works even if you are setting an in and an out yourself and there is a scene break in the middle. If it is left on, automatic scene detection will break your capture at each detected scene change, whether you want it to or not.

To choose to capture only audio or only video, use the wing menu in the Capture window and choose "record Video" or "Record Audio" as appropriate. Scene detection and capture settings are also available from the Capture window wing menu.

Importing Files

There will be times when you need to bring a file into Premiere Pro that already exists on your hard drive. Video clips, audio clips, and graphics can be imported into the Project window by using the pulldown File ▶ Import, or by using the keyboard command, which is Ctrl + I. Alternatively, you can right-click in a blank space in the Project window and select Import from the context menu.

Toward the bottom of the Import dialogue, the File of type pop-up will display a list of compatible file types when you click on the down arrow. For easier sorting, you may want to select from the list the type of file you're searching for. This will only show you that type of file and folder in the browser.

Premiere Pro can import many types of media, including the files output by many other Adobe applications. See Chapter 11 for further details on how Premiere Pro handles these files.

ORGANIZING YOUR MEDIA

One of the more significant concepts involved in working with the media inside Adobe Premiere Pro is that the Project window is not a directory, or a folder as you would see on your hard drive when you sort files and group them. The items you see in the Project window are *links* to the content you are using and to its original location. Editing, renaming, or even deleting a file from the Project window will have no effect on the original media file on disk.

On the other hand, if you move or delete a file from your hard drive that is involved in a Premiere Pro project, this will cause Premiere Pro to see it as missing, and you will be asked to find it the next time you open the project.

The Project window with sequences, bins, and source media.

The Project window is not only a list of your clips, graphics, and audio, it's also a tool to sort and organize those resources, so that you can find elements quickly and efficiently.

Media can be organized into groups through the use of *bins*. Bins appear in the Project window as folders. You can create a new bin by right-clicking in an empty spot in the Project window and selecting New Bin or by clicking on the folder icon at the bottom of the Project window. Delete a

The Parent Bin button.

bin and its contents by selecting the bin and pressing the Delete key, or by selecting the bin and clicking the Delete icon (the trash can) at the bottom of the Project window.

These folders can contain any source clips or sequences, or even more bins. You can place existing media into a bin by dragging the item over the new target bin and dropping the clip onto it. You can also import into the bin you have open.

When you need to go back to a bin's parent directory—the bin or the root directory that the bin is inside—use the Parent Bin button, which is just above the clip area of the Project window, on the left side.

Viewing Clips

As you select a clip in the Project window, the first frame of the clip will show up in the header portion of the window, called the *thumbnail viewer*. Information about the clip, such as the duration, audio sample rate, and frame size and pixel aspect ratio, will show up beside the video picture.

Thumbnail Viewer

You may have cases where the first frame of the clip isn't visually significant enough to help you recognize the clip. To select another frame to appear in the icon, you need to set a *poster frame*. To set a poster frame, follow these steps:

1 Select the clip in a Project window.

2 Drag the slider below the video frame in the thumbnail viewer to shuttle the clip, or click on the Play button to the left of the video frame.

3 When the frame you want is displayed, click on the Set Poster Frame button, which is above the Play/Stop button to the left of the video frame (it looks like a small camera).

The Set Poster Frame button.

Displaying and Sorting Items in the Project Window

The Project window has two basic options for layout: the Icon view and the List view.

Project window Icon view.

Project window List view.

List view button

Icon view button

The views can be toggled in two ways. The first (and I think the easiest) way is to click on the Icon and List view buttons at the bottom of the Project window. The second way is to go into the Project wing menu and select View ▶ Icon or View ▶ List.

The advantage to the Icon view is that it's very visual; the drawback can be that only a limited number of items fit into view at one time. The size of the thumbnails can be changed in the Project window wing menu by selecting Thumbnails ▶ (small/medium/large).

The advantage to List view is that far more information is displayed and far more items are up in the Project window. The disadvantage is that you have to click on each clip to see a preview in the thumbnail viewer to get a visual idea of what the content might be.

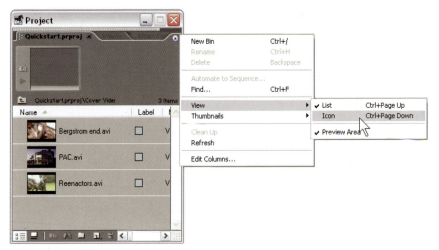

Icon and List view options in the Project window menu.

Using the Project Window to Storyboard

The Icon view can be used to visually arrange, or *storyboard*, clips in preparation for editing them into a sequence. Moving clips, by dragging any clip to any square, will rearrange the clips. If there is already a clip in the destination position, you will need to watch the indicator to determine where you will be inserting the moved clip. Between the two clips, where the moved clip will be inserted, the border will turn thicker and black when you drag over it. It behaves a bit like a word processor: when you insert more material, it pushes the existing material out of the way to make room. After you've finished rearranging your clips, select Clean Up from the Project window wing menu to delete empty spaces.

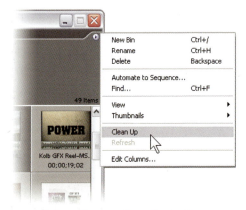

Select Clean Up from the Project window menu to eliminate empty space in the Icon view.

After rearranging clips in the Icon view (or just selecting a series of clips from the List view), you can automatically lay the series of clips onto the timeline with the Automate to Sequence feature.

1 Select a continuous series of clips by clicking on the first clip and Shift-clicking on the last, or select a noncontinuous series of clips by clicking on the first one and Control-clicking on each additional clip. Or simply use Edit ▶ Select All if you want to select all the clips in a bin.

2 Click the Automate to Sequence button at the bottom of the Project window.

3 Choose the proper options from the dialogue.

The dialogue will offer you the option of taking the clips in their order in the bin (sort order) or, in the case of a noncontinuous group, in the order in which you selected them.

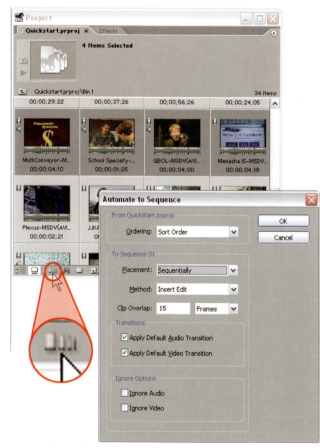

The Automate to Sequence button and dialogue.

You can also choose to lay them down sequentially end-to-end or to place them at unnumbered markers. After choosing whether to insert or overlay (insert and overlay are discussed in detail in Chapter 5 on page 66) and how much clip overlap you want, you can lay the series of clips down, with your default video and audio transitions already applied if you wish.

You have an extensive set of options for sorting your clips in the List view. The columns to the right of the clip name hold the information you need to rearrange your clips based on any of the headings.

The first thing you will want to do is to determine which of these columns is really important to you, then turn the rest off. By selecting Edit Columns from the Project window wing menu, you will bring up a dialogue that will allow you to choose which columns to display and, through the use of Move Up or Move Down, to reorder them.

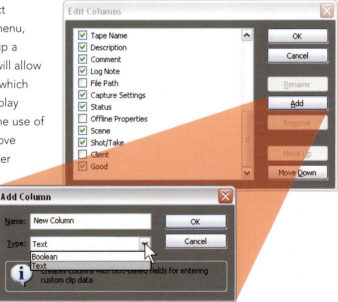

The Edit Columns and Add Column dialogues.

You can also create custom columns from the Edit Columns dialogue by clicking on Add. You will need to name your column and decide between Text and Boolean column types. Text will create a column that accepts text you key in, and Boolean creates a column with a checkbox.

Click and drag the borders between columns to change their width.

You can also reorder the columns by dragging the headers to a new position in the Project window. You can change the width of the columns by dragging the borders between the headers.

To sort clips via the List view, you can click on the header of the column that represents the criteria you would like to sort. If you want to see what clips are used in the timeline, click on the Video Usage column. If you want to see which clips aren't used in the timeline, clicking the column header again reverses the order, bringing the unused clips to the top.

To rename a clip, do the following:

1 Click once on the clip name, then click again.

2 You'll notice that the name becomes highlighted. Type the new name, and press Enter or Return.

As we discussed earlier, the name change in the Project window does not change the name of the media file on disk. If you change the names of your clips frequently, it may be a good idea to keep a record of the original filenames, in case you need to find a certain file on disk.

Deleting an Item

To delete an item from the Project window, select the clip and press the Delete key or right-click the item and select Clear from the context menu.

To clear unused clips in List view, you will want to have the Video Usage

# of instances of each clip on the timeline

and Audio Usage columns active and in view, then do a sort by clicking the appropriate column header. Select and delete the clips that aren't used in the timeline.

If you want to delete the clip from the project and its media file from your hard drive, you can right-click on a clip and select Unlink Media from the context menu. You will be given a choice of whether or not to delete the media file from the hard drive.

Search Function

To find an item in the Project window, use the Find button (the binoculars symbol) at the bottom of the window. The Find dialogue will come up. You can specify two parameters based on the column headings, specify the options, and click Find. If you need to search the entire project, make sure that you are currently in the root directory. Search will scan subfolders but targets its search based on the bin currently selected.

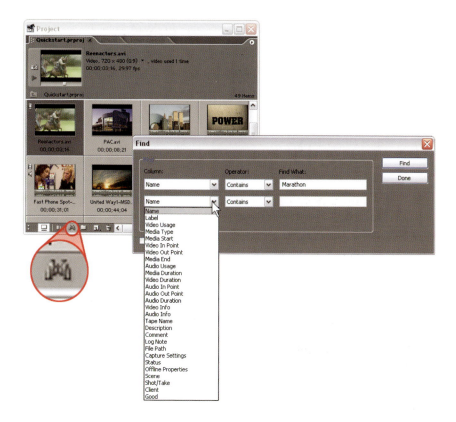

MONITORS

The Monitor window has two sections: the Source view on the left, and the Program (or Sequence) view on the right.

The Monitor window.

I like to think of the Source view as a "prep" area. The typical workflow will find an editor taking a clip from the Project window into the Source Monitor to decide what section of the clip to use, then setting in and out points before editing it into the timeline.

The Program view is the playback of your timeline, or your edit. Many of us, who have been around since video editing involved only video decks, might refer to this monitor as the "record" monitor—like the monitor we used to view our completed edits played back on the record VTR.

A clip is brought into the Source view by dragging it out of the Project window into the Source Monitor, or by simply double-clicking a clip in the Project window or on the timeline. The Program view is actually the visual playback of the timeline and shows the frame that the current time indicator (CTI) is currently on, whether playing back or paused.

Although these two monitors have slightly different roles to play, there are some things that we can address right away which hold true for both.

The Transport controls at the bottom of each window control playback like a VCR. You can play, rewind, fast forward, and stop. The thumbwheel and slider can shuttle and *jog* (frame-by-frame) through a clip or sequence.

Both monitors have several options available from the wing menu.

There is a wing menu for both the Source Monitor and the Sequence Monitor.

Test Displays

If you are editing DV for personal use on videotape or for playback on a computer, chances are that your video doesn't require a lot of adjustment if you choose not to do so. However, in the world of video and television engineering, the video signal must be tightly regulated. To monitor the technical aspects of the video signal, test displays, such as waveform monitors and vectorscopes, are utilized. Although the concepts of reading waveform monitors and vectorscopes could easily fill this book, there are some basics that users at almost every level can employ to make the test displays useful.

In the waveform monitor, you will notice a grid displayed that shows values from approximately –30 to +130. The negative values come from analog video engineering and are only there for two reasons: to make the test display familiar to professionals and to represent color saturation in darker areas of the picture. The part of the grid to focus on is the area between 0 and 100. You always want your video to be between these two numbers so that your digital video won't *clip*. Clipping occurs when certain picture values exceed what can be shown. When you see values in your footage that exceed these boundaries, you may need to make some adjustments. Look for the lavender-colored line along the right edge of the display for the actual luminance range of your picture—very saturated colors can produce waveform over 100 due to the color (as opposed to the luminance) level or saturation, which may not make them "illegal."

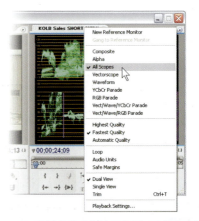

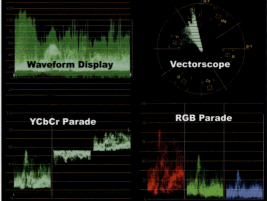

The test displays are available from the wing menu. An enlarged version of each of the four test signals is pictured, along with the actual video frame they are displaying.

The vectorscope has a different job from the waveform: its primary job is measuring color saturation and phase—you might think of it as "tint." The distance from the center out is the amount of color saturation. The direction in which the waveform grows from the center indicates the phase, or just what color the color is.

An outer ring on the vectorscope display represents the limit of acceptable color saturation. If your video causes a vectorscope display outside the circle, you have a color that is too saturated for broadcast. You can identify which color is the problem by seeing where the color displays on the vectorscope display. There is a pie slice–shaped zone each for blue, cyan, green, yellow, red, and magenta: all the colors you would normally see in a test pattern display. Portions of your image that have no color saturation, such as white, gray, or black, show up as a dot in the center.

The YCbCr Parade and RGB Parade signals display the relative values of your image based on three color components of analog video. These are YCbCr (Y = Luminance, Cb = Chroma Blue component, Cr = Chroma Red component), also sometimes referred to as *YUV*, or the three base components of your computer display: red, green, blue (RGB). These displays can be used to do technical color correction or to track colors that are outside of acceptable limits.

If you want to learn more about how to understand these signals, refer to a publication such as *Video Color Correction for Nonlinear Editors*, by Stuart Blake Jones (Focal Press, 2003; ISBN: 0-240-80515-1) for details.

To access the test displays, do the following:

1   Move your cursor over the wing menu button located in the top right corner of the Program or Source Monitor.

2   Click the left mouse button to open the menu.

3   Drag the mouse onto the menu over the test monitor option you would like to select.

4   The selected test display will appear in the appropriate monitor. To return to video, simply reopen the menu and select Composite.

In the case of the Program Monitor, you can also create a new, floating monitor window for test display by selecting New Reference Monitor. The new window

that opens
will have the
same options
for video and
test signal
monitoring
as the two
monitors in
the original
Monitor
window. The
Reference
Monitor can
be nested in
the Source
side of the
Monitor window, if you wish.

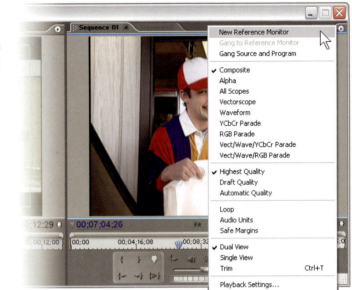

"Ganging" a Reference Monitor to the Program Monitor

You can link the new floating monitor to the program monitor so that both overlay windows update simultaneously. This may be useful when you would like to view the video picture in one window while viewing the video's test display in another. The steps that follow describe how to link, or *gang,* the new reference monitor to the program output.

After you've created the new reference monitor

1   Click on the Wing menu button in the top right corner of the Reference Monitor window to open the wing menu.

2   Choose Gang to Program Monitor.

3   The monitor will now reference the same video as the Program Monitor.

4   You can also gang the Program Monitor to the new Reference Monitor through its wing menu, selecting Gang to Reference Monitor.

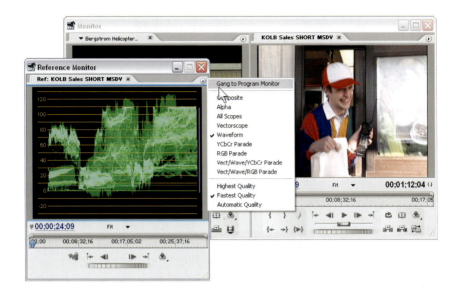

Once you've ganged a Reference Monitor, you will notice that updating each overlay window simultaneously will affect the real-time playback of your footage. To resume real-time playback and preview, close the Reference Monitor or select Gang to Program Monitor again, to deselect it.

Loop

The source clip or the program sequence can be set to loop the video between the in point and the out point, making it easier to scrutinize details than by constantly backing up and pressing Play. A clip or sequence can be set to loop through the wing menu or by clicking on the Loop button below the video picture in the Monitor window.

Audio Units

When you select Audio Units, the timeline switches from hours: minutes: seconds: frames to audio samples, making it easier and more precise to work with audio elements.

Quality Settings

Depending on your system, you may want to adjust the quality of the video overlay on the desktop. The three settings are Highest Quality, Fastest Quality, and Automatic Quality. The Highest setting gives you the best-quality image but will tax slower systems. Fastest Quality lowers the overlay quality of your image (not the actual video) in areas where the software must render a preview, as in the case of transitions or applied video filters. Automatic Quality senses the capability of your system and adjusts accordingly. Each monitor (Source and Program) has its own quality setting in its wing menu.

Safe Areas

You can display a 10% and 20% safe window to show safe action and safe title windows over the video picture. These traditionally indicate safe composition for all television sets. The percentages can be changed in the Project Settings dialogue box. Safe areas can be applied

The Safe Margins button in the Monitor window.

through the wing menu or by clicking on the Safe Margins button below the video picture in the Monitor window.

Dual View and Single View

You can make the Monitor window even smaller by choosing to display only one view. If you choose Single View from the wing menu in the Source view, only the Source view will stay open. The Program view will remain open if you're selecting from the Program view wing menu.

Many times, an editor may decide to use an NTSC video monitor as a program monitor and cut down to only the Source view on the computer display. Other times, the Source view may not be necessary and you can free up space by closing it (for example, if you're mixing audio).

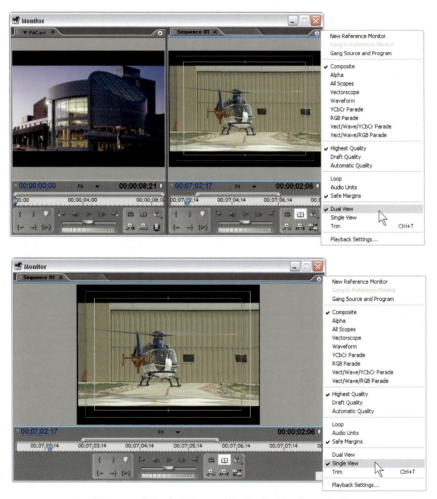

Dual View and Single View modes in the Monitor window.

Preparing a Clip in the Source Monitor

The source monitor is often used to preview and mark in and out points on clips before bringing them to the timeline. Here's how to use the Source Monitor to prepare a clip:

1   Double-click on a clip in the Project window or drag a clip to the Source window.

2   Below the video window, you will notice a timeline with a blue cursor, or CTI.

3   Move the CTI until the video frame shows the point in the clip that you want to be the in point.

4   Below the left side of the timeline, you will notice two brackets. The open bracket ({) is to choose the in point. Click on it (or press the *I* key), and you will notice that the darker, blue-tinted stripe in the timeline shortens, to start at your newly selected in point.

5   By positioning the CTI at your desired out point and selecting the close bracket (}) (or pressing the *O* key), you've now marked in and out points on your clip.

Set Out Point Button
Set In Point Button

The Set In Point and Set Out Point buttons and a clip showing in and out points.

At this point, you can drag the prepared clip from your Source view to your timeline—but we're going to cover that in much more detail in Chapter 6.

EDITING

Sometimes, with all the options, interface functionality, and project setup information, it can be easy to forget that what we're supposed to be doing here is cutting video, audio, and graphic content together.

In some ways, editing video and audio is a strange process. Since the days of the film editor with a razor blade and bins full of film clips, the very object of editing has been to discard and to create: destruction and construction. Raw material must be evaluated and sorted, then the chosen pieces, minus the parts that have been cut away, are put together to create a finished product.

For those readers who are new to editing video using a computer, it is a bit like using a word processor to write a letter or a report. Attempting to choose the right words carefully, you write a sentence, then you review it. As you reconsider the phrasing, you decide to add a word in one, which that makes the entire sentence longer; in another instance you decide to replace one word with another, and at yet another point in the sentence you decide to discard a word completely.

The same methods can be employed with video and audio. The largest difference is that a writer has all the words in a known language at his or her disposal, whereas a video editor has the video shots and audio clips he or she has been given. The shots are viewed, assembled in a preliminary sequence, and then rearranged and removed, replaced and revised.

This chapter covers the slicing, dicing, arranging, and rearranging that are actually video editing.

If we carry the word processor analogy a bit further, in English, text is read from left to right. In Premiere Pro, you will notice the video and audio are played from left to right when represented on a timeline. Inserting a word into a sentence pushes the existing words to the right. Inserting video into an existing sequence can be done in the same way, pushing existing footage to the right. Each track in the Timeline window is like a line of text. The major departure from the printed page is there is no right margin, and Premiere Pro reads all the lines at once.

The work area for our assembly of the program is the Timeline window. The Timeline window contains *tracks*, which are the organization system for your content on the timeline, creating something a bit like a graph of your program over time. You have multiple tracks of video and audio (99 of each should you need them) that each flow from left to right over time.

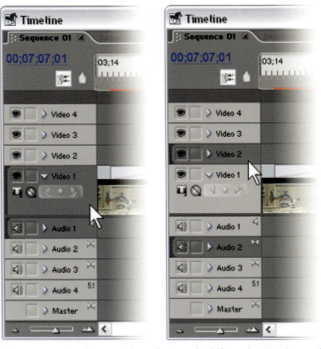

The Timeline window.

Targeting Tracks

With all these different tracks, performing operations on your timeline can get confusing. As we start to address functions in the timeline, the concept of *targeting* tracks should probably be our first stop.

Two examples of targeted tracks. On the left, Video Track 1 and Audio Track 1 are targeted. On the right, Video Track 2 and Audio Track 2 are targeted.

When a track is targeted, it means that particular track is chosen for certain operations (more on what these operations are a bit later). To target a track, click in the track header area at the far left of the Sequence window, in the space where the name of the track is located. The space will darken as the track is selected. You can unselect a selected track by clicking in the track header area again.

Insert and Overlay Editing

The second important concept is the idea that when you place a clip in the timeline, there are two basic ways to apply it to your sequence: insert and overlay.

Insert goes with our word processor metaphor, as you might expect. When you insert a word into a sentence, the words that come after it must move over to allow it some space, creating a longer sentence. The same thing holds true for your timeline. Inserting a shot will make all the clips on the track, or on the entire timeline, move over to allow space.

Overlay is more like selecting a certain word, or group of words, and typing something in to replace it. The text you selected doesn't move down; it is replaced, or overwritten. Overlay editing differs from insert editing because it doesn't move anything down; it just drops the new clip on top of whatever is currently occupying that space, overlaying or "overwriting" it, effectively eliminating the material that was originally in that position.

There are several ways to insert or overlay edit a clip into your sequence. You can preview a clip in the Source window and use the Insert or the Overlay button to place the clip in your sequence, with the in point at the position of the current time indicator (CTI), into the target track(s) on the timeline.

The alternative is to drag the clip from the Source window (or directly from the Project window) to the position in the sequence where you would like it. The track in the timeline on which you intend to place the clip can be considered your *destination track*. By simply dragging the clip to the destination track in the timeline, you will perform an overlay edit. This is the default behavior.

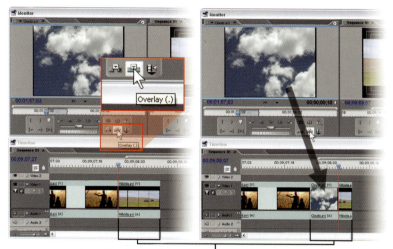

In an Overlay edit, the clip on the timeline does not move
but gets covered by the new clip.

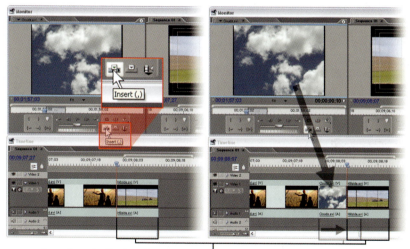

In an Insert edit, the clip on the timeline is displaced by the inserted clip.

An insert edit and an overlay edit from the source window. Note that the new clip
will go to the CTI position in the *targeted track(s)*.

There are two ways to insert a clip, both involving modifier keys. You can insert
on the timeline, creating a gap in all the tracks in your timeline, or you can
choose simply to shift the destination track(s).

1 To insert a clip and shift all tracks, drag the clip holding down the Control key (Ctrl).

2 If you want to shift only the destination track(s), hold down Ctrl+Alt while dragging your clip.

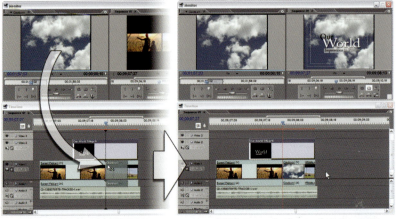

Drag a clip to the timeline with no modifier keys to do an Overlay edit.

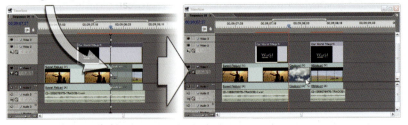

Drag a clip to the timeline holding the Control key to insert and shift all tracks. Notice that clips that span the insert point on nondestination tracks are split apart at the insert "in" point, creating a gap in those tracks equal to the inserted clip.

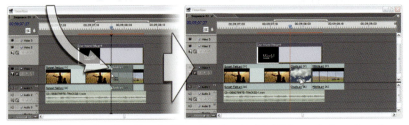

Drag a clip to the timeline holding the Control + Alt keys to insert and shift only the destination track.

The modifier keys for shifting target track(s) and all tracks will also work with the Insert button in the Source view.

Note: Shifting only the destination track(s) can cause unintended consequences later in the timeline. Video, audio, and graphic material residing on several tracks and properly positioned in relation to each other will not move together. When doing an insert into a complex program, I usually find that the clean-up work necessary to take care of split clips (and any other consequences of inserting and shifting all tracks) is still much easier than tracking down and correcting all the possible errors down the timeline caused by shifting only destination tracks.

Modifying In and Out Points on the Source Clip

To alter the in and out points of your raw clip, you can double-click on the raw clip in the timeline, and the raw clip will open in the Source view to mark or change an in and out points. Or you can trim the clip on the timeline.

To set in and out points in the Source view, take these steps:

1. Double click (or drag) a clip into the Source view.

2. Using the shuttle or jog controls below the Source Monitor, or the JKL keys, position the clip at your desired in point.

3. Click the Set In Point button in the source window, or simply press the I key.

4. Using the shuttle or jog controls below the Source Monitor, or the JKL keys, position the clip at your desired out point.

5 Click the Set Out Point button in the Source window, or simply press the O key.

Trimming Clips in the Sequence

To trim a clip after you've placed it in your sequence, do the following:

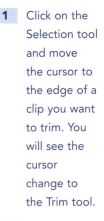

Trimming a Clip

Click and drag the edge of a clip to change its length.

Release and the clip is the new length.

Trimming a Clip on an Edit Point

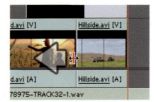

This trim will affect the clip to the right of the cut.

This trim will affect the clip to the left of the cut.

1 Click on the Selection tool and move the cursor to the edge of a clip you want to trim. You will see the cursor change to the Trim tool.

2 The Trim tool will show a bracket facing the edge of the clip it will trim. If you are working near a cut, you may have to adjust the positioning slightly to ensure you are trimming the correct clip.

3 To trim the audio or video portion of a clip only, while not affecting the trims of the other part, hold the Alt key while trimming the video or audio part of the clip.

Three-Point Editing

Three-point editing is a technique for which only three of the four possible edit points are specified (the four edit points include an in point and an out point on the source and an in point and an out point on the timeline). Three-point edits are one of the most common operations in editing. You can do three-point editing with Premiere Pro by selecting an in point and/or an out point on your source clip and doing the following:

1 Position the CTI in the Timeline window at the point where you wish to start the new shot. Press the I key or select the In Point button in the Program view.

2 Or you can position the CTI in the Timeline window at the point where you wish to end the new shot. Press the O key or select the Out Point button in the Sequence Monitor.

You can perform steps 1 and 2 if you only have one point selected on your source clip.

3 Click the Insert or the Overlay button in the Source Monitor to complete the edit.

Note: By setting the in and out points for both the source and the sequence, you will have what is called a *four-point edit*. Unless the time lengths defined by each set of ins and outs are identical, traditionally, the source clip would be sped up or slowed down to fill the gap properly. This is sometimes referred to as a *fit-to-fill* edit.

Premiere Pro will sense when the source and record settings are of different lengths and present you with options for how you would like to complete the edit.

An example of a three-point edit. There is a source in point, a source out point, and a record or timeline in point. If the timeline had a specified out point, it would be considered a four-point edit.

The Tool Palette

The tools in the Tool palette are the "bread and butter" functions of video editing.

- **The Horse:** He doesn't do anything. You could right-click on him to choose whether to display the palette horizontally or vertically, but otherwise he (or she) is for decoration only.

- **Selection tool:** This is the tool you will be using most often. You can choose, select, and drag items in the various windows in Premiere Pro. This is the tool you will use to interact with buttons and controls throughout the interface.

- **Track Select tool:** This tool is designed to enable you to select everything from the point of selection forward in a track and slide it down. The relationship between the clips that are selected doesn't change. By using this tool with the Shift key, you can select everything from a point forward in all tracks.

- **Ripple Edit tool:** We'll address ripple editing on page 82.

- **Rolling Edit tool:** We'll address rolling edits on page 82.

- **Rate Stretch tool:** Use this tool to stretch or compress the duration of a clip on the timeline. This tool can be used as a sort of manual fit-to-fill tool if you have a clip trimmed on the timeline and you need to adjust it to fill a gap.

- **Razor tool:** Oddly enough, this tool cuts things. If you need to separate a clip into two parts while it's on the timeline, you can cut it into multiple parts using the Razor tool. Many editors will capture a very long piece of footage and cut it up on the timeline. By using this tool with the Shift key, you can create a cut in one place through the clips on all tracks.

- **Slip tool:** We'll discuss slip editing on page 80.

- **Slide tool:** We'll discuss slide editing on page 80.

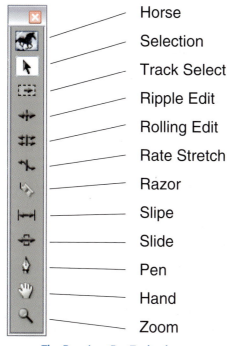

Horse

Selection

Track Select

Ripple Edit

Rolling Edit

Rate Stretch

Razor

Slipe

Slide

Pen

Hand

Zoom

The Premiere Pro Tool palette.

- **Pen tool:** This tool is used on the timeline to adjust volume and opacity. We'll discuss the Pen tool on page 98.

- **Hand tool:** This tool is used primarily for sliding views in windows, for instance, to drag the sequence display to the right or left to view a different portion of the program.

- **Zoom tool:** You guessed it. This tool "zooms" you in and out to do more detailed work or to get a wider overview in windows, such as the Timeline window and the Effect Controls window.

Cut, Copy, and Paste

Cutting and copying of clips can be done by selecting a clip, right-clicking, and selecting Copy or Cut from the context menu. Or you can select the clip and type Ctrl + C to copy the clip, or Ctrl + X to cut it. To paste, position the CTI on the timeline and make sure to target the track(s) where you want the new clip to go. Then, use the Edit ▶ Paste command or Ctrl + V to paste the clip into the targeted track at the CTI.

| Click on the clip you want to copy, then press Ctrl + C. | Press Ctrl + V to paste at the CTI. Note that the pasted clip and its associated audio went to the chosen target tracks. |

Excluding and Locking Tracks

If you are working with several layers of video and graphics or many tracks of audio, you will have occasions when you don't need to see all the layers at once to do the task at hand. In these cases, you can improve Premiere Pro's performance and reduce the visual or audible clutter for yourself by disabling, or *excluding*, one or several tracks.

To exclude a track, click on the Toggle Track Output button on the far left side of the Timeline window. For video tracks, this would be the symbol that looks like an eye; for audio tracks, the button resembles a small speaker. In each case, the symbol will disappear when a track is disabled.

After a portion of your project has been edited, you may want to *lock* an entire track to preserve your work against accidental changes.

The Toggle
Track Output buttons

The Toggle
Track Lock buttons
(Note the Crosshatch
on the locked tracks.)

To lock a track, click in the square space next to the eye or speaker symbol in the track header at the far left of the Timeline window. This is the Toggle Track Lock button. When a track is locked, the clips should all have a crosshatch pattern across them, and you will see a padlock icon visible on the toggle button.

Linked and Unlinked Clips

When you bring a clip that has audio and video components to the timeline, the two parts of the clip will appear on the appropriate tracks. However, the two parts of the clip will respond to modification together. Trimming or dragging either clip will result in identical results for both clips. The two components are said to be *linked*.

If you need to separate the audio from the video to work with each component on its own, you need to *unlink* them. There are two ways to unlink a clip:

- Select the clip. From the pulldown, go to Clip ► Unlink Audio and Video.

- Or right-click the clip and select Unlink Audio and Video from the context menu.

Right-click on the clips and choose Unlink Audio and Video to unlink the audio and video portions of a clip.

After unlinking a clip, click off the clip in a blank area of the timeline and click back to one portion of the clip to deselect the pair and make a change to the audio or video individually.

Even after the clips have been unlinked, Premiere Pro will still remember that they belong together and will tell you if they are out of sync and, if you relink them, how many frames the offset is.

Relinking Clips

To relink two clips that have been previously unlinked, follow these steps:

1 Select the first part of the clip, either video or audio.

2 Shift-select the second clip.

3 From the pulldown menu, select Clip ▶ Link Audio and Video.

4 Or you can right-click on either clip and select Link Audio and Video.

Right-click on the clip and choose Link Audio and Video to link an audio and a video clip.

You may also want to link clips that weren't previously linked. This can be handy when you've aligned some footage to specific audio and you now want to keep the relationship between the two clips constant. To link the two clips, follow the relinking procedure just described.

Note: You can't link two audio clips or two video clips together. Neither can you link more than one audio clip to one video clip or multiple video clips to one audio clip.

Bringing Video and Audio Clips Back into Sync

When you have an audio and a video clip out of synchronization, Premiere Pro will give you the number of frames (or more extensive seconds, minutes, etc.), provided the two clips are linked. The offset will appear to the left of the clip name with a + or – to indicate the direction of offset. Resync the clips by right-clicking on the offset number and choosing one of the following:

> **Move into Sync:** This option will move the part of the clip you clicked to a position where it syncs with the other portion (right-click on the video clip's offset and it will move to the audio clip's position, or click on the audio to move to the position of the video clip).

Note: When you select Move into Sync, if there is a clip occupying the position needed by the synchronizing clip, the synchronizing clip will overlay the clip that's in its way.

> **Slip into Sync:** This option will not move the clip but will change the trim points so that the audio and video are synchronized, even though they may have different in and out points.

You can also slide the clip into sync manually by holding down the Alt key and dragging the part of the clip you want to move.

Moving Edits in the Sequence

The fine (and even not-so-fine) adjustments of editing can be made in the Sequence window. Most of the work in the Sequence window can be done by using the Selection tool to drag clips and by using the Slip and Slide tools to adjust cut points.

To move a clip in the sequence with the mouse, click and drag it along the timeline. It's important to note that the default behavior for the clip you're

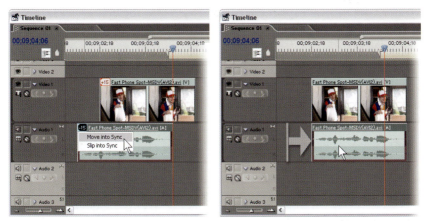

Move into Sync will move the clip into sync with its linked footage or sound. Note that the clip that is clicked on is the one that moves.

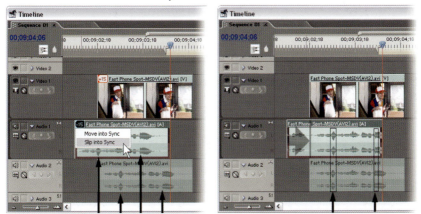

(Note the relative position of the content.)

(Audio is now synchronous even though the in and out points have not moved.)

Slip into Sync will move the content into sync but will not move the in and out points. A version of the audio in sync is included here on Audio 2 for reference.

moving is to overlay. If you should cause utter destruction when this slips your mind (as it does mine occasionally), make sure to undo using Ctrl + Z, because simply moving the clip back will leave a gap. (See page 66 for further information on insert and overlay.)

Slip and Slide Adjustments

You can also edit clips in the timeline by using the Slip and Slide tools in the Tool palette.

The difference between the Slip and Slide tools is essentially the difference between shifting the in and out trim points on the source clip with the Slip tool and changing the in and out points on the timeline with the Slide tool.

When you click and drag a clip after selecting either the Slip or the Slide tool, you will notice that the display in the monitor changes. The

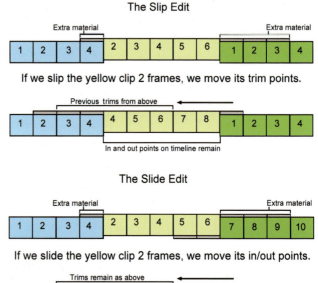

The Slip Edit

If we slip the yellow clip 2 frames, we move its trim points.

The Slide Edit

If we slide the yellow clip 2 frames, we move its in/out points.

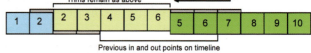

Program view will show you four images: the last frame of the previous clip, the first and last frames of the selected clip, and the first frame of the next clip—basically, the two edits that involve your selected clip. These frames have two different arrangements, depending on which tool you're using. The images that are changing with the adjustment are always the largest ones.

This concept is more difficult to grasp through words than it is by seeing it for yourself. I'd encourage you to experiment with Slip and Slide to become more familiar with the techniques.

When using the Slip tool, you will notice that the first and last frames of your selected clip are the largest pictures and that they are changing while the preceding clip's last frame and succeeding clip's first frame, which do not

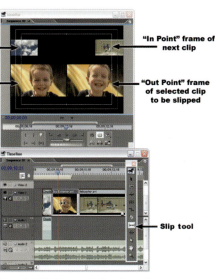

"Out Point" frame of the preceeding clip

"In Point" frame of next clip

"In Point" frame of selected clip to be slipped

"Out Point" frame of selected clip to be slipped

Slip tool

The Slip tool with its specialized monitor.

change, show as smaller frames above. This is because you are affecting which part of the clip we see, not where it is positioned on the timeline.

The Slide tool will cause the frame sizes to be reversed. Because you are changing the preceding out point and the succeeding in point, those frames are now largest, and the selected clip's first and last frames are smaller and do not change. This is because you are now moving the clip on the timeline, affecting the clips around your selected clip, not changing which part of the clip is seen.

"In Point" frame of selected clip to slide

"Out Point" frame of selected clip to slide

"Out Point" frame of the preceeding clip

"In Point" frame of next clip

Slide tool

The Slide tool with its specialized monitor.

Ripple and Roll Adjustments

Unlike the Slip and Slide tools, which are designed to move clips, the Ripple and Rolling Edit tools are designed to move edit points.

Note: You must have some extra material available beyond the trim points of your clips for the Ripple and Rolling Edit tools to be fully functional.

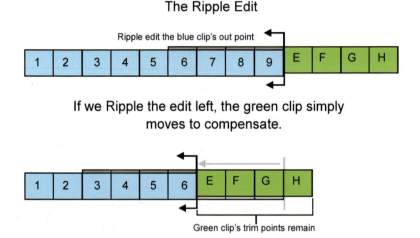

The Ripple Edit

Ripple edit the blue clip's out point

If we Ripple the edit left, the green clip simply moves to compensate.

Green clip's trim points remain

The Ripple Edit tool will actually move an edit point by affecting the clip you are adjusting and by moving the entire timeline after that point to fill the gap or allow extra space, based on your adjustment. This ultimately lengthens or shortens your entire edited sequence.

The Rolling Edit tool will move an edit point in time, trimming one clip while expanding the adjacent clip, ultimately keeping the edited sequence exactly the same length through this method of give and take.

The Trim Window

There are times when an edit needs fine adjustments. It can be much easier to fine-tune an edit if you can see the frames you are cutting on and can try some variations. This is where the Trim window comes in handy.

The Rolling Edit

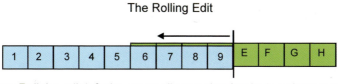

If we Roll the edit left, the green clip remains, but its in point moves.

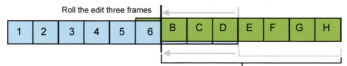

Roll the edit three frames

In and out points on timeline have changed.

(Bottom of the Program View)

Go to Last/Next Edit

Trim Window button

The Trim Window

Jog Out Point   Roll the Cut Point   Jog In Point

Cut Point

To use the Trim window, position the CTI directly on an edit point. This can be done by using the Page Up and Page Down keys, or by using the Next Edit and Last Edit buttons in the Monitor window. Once you are positioned on an edit, click on the Trim button, or press Ctrl + T. The Trim window will open with two panes, like the Monitor window, and it may open directly over the Monitor window. The Trim window does not replace your Monitor window, which you can view either by dragging the Trim window to a different position or by simply closing it when you're done.

Once the window is open, you will notice three thumbwheels in the bottom center of the window. The one on the left jogs the out point of the clip before the cut, the wheel in the center rolls the edit, and the wheel on the right jogs the in point of the clip that comes after the cut. These functions can also be accomplished by clicking and dragging in each monitor pane. When you click and drag on the border in between the monitors, you can roll the edit.

Split Edits

Split edits are when the audio and video parts of a clip have different in and out points. Many times, when editors are cutting a dramatic performance, perhaps a conversation taking place between two actors, there are times when the picture needs to cut at a different point than the sound. Perhaps Actor #1 says something shocking and we want to see the look on Actor #2's face before he responds verbally, but also before Actor #1 has delivered his entire line, even though we need to hear all of it. In this case, we cut picture first to catch the visible reaction, then cut sound as Actor #1 finishes talking and Actor #2 starts to respond.

This is called a *split edit*. The popular forms of this are the *J cut,* where the audio in point is ahead of the video in point, and the *L cut,* where the audio out point trails the video out point. The letter nicknames for the edits come from visualizing the "shape" of the edit—and our industry's ever-increasing need for additional technical jargon.

Although you can set different in and out points for video and audio in the Source view before moving the clip to the timeline, the most effective way to do this is when the clips are already "rough cut" together on the timeline.

To be able to perform a split edit, it's important that you have extra trim material available outside of the clips' current in and out points.

1 Select the
Rolling Edit
tool.

2 Use the tool on
either the video
or audio track,
holding down
the Alt key.

The aptly named "J" and "L" cuts

Use the Rolling edit Tool with the Alt key to Roll the
audio portion of the edit.

If you then use the Selection tool and trim the clip (without the
Alt key), both parts of the clip trim together.

3   The track you adjust will be independent of its companion track. However, if you attempt to roll edit or simply trim that clip later, without using the Alt key, the in or out points will move proportionately to each other.

You can trim the audio and video portions of a clip separately by using the trim method, described earlier, with the Alt key.

Selecting Multiple Items on the Timeline

Use one of the following methods to select multiple items on the timeline:

- Select the first clip and Shift-click on the additional clips.

- Or click and drag a marquee box over the group of clips you'd like to select.

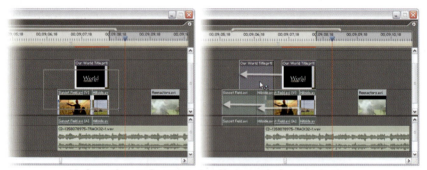

Using the select tool, click and drag a box, touching all the clips you want to select. Then click and drag the selected group.

Creating New Sequences

The Timeline window contains your edited sequences. Each sequence is a self-contained edit "timeline" in itself. Multiple sequences are useful for creating multiple versions of your program or *subtimelines*, where each segment of your program can be worked on separately and multiple sequences assembled in an additional master sequence.

You can create a new, empty sequence document by selecting File ▶ New ▶ Sequence.

There may be times when you edit a program, and then you decide that you would like to try an

alternate version of your edited sequence, but you don't want to destroy what you've done. You can do this by creating a duplicate of your sequence and making the changes to the duplicate, while keeping your original sequence intact.

Here's how to make a duplicate of an existing sequence to create an alternate version of your program:

1 In the Project window, find the sequence you want to duplicate.

Right-click on the sequence you want to duplicate and select Duplicate from the context menu.

2 Right-click on the sequence and select Duplicate from the context menu.

3 You will create a new sequence called *<original name> copy*.

4 If you wish, right-click on the new sequence and give it a new name.

Slow and Fast Motion

You can adjust the speed of a clip in Premiere Pro. To put a clip into *slow-motion* or *fast-motion*, you can do any one of the following:

• Click on the clip, go to the Clip ▶ Speed Duration pulldown menu, and type a percentage in the dialogue.

   Specify a new duration in the dialogue.

• Right-click on the clip in the timeline and select Speed/Duration from the context menu and type a new percentage.

   Specify a new duration.

Right-click on your clip and select Speed/Duration from the context menu.

Or, the last option:

- Use the Rate Stretch tool to alter the speed of a clip on the timeline. When you drag the tool on the outer edge of a clip, the Rate Stretch tool will lengthen or shorten the clip by time-expanding or compressing the material. This tool works similarly to trimming, except you are time-expanding or compressing the content, not adding or subtracting material.

Note: If you want a clip to run backward, click the Reverse Speed checkbox and enter a percentage or duration.

Speeding up a video clip will also speed its associated audio, making human speech begin to sound like a squeaky toy for dogs. Or, when the clip is slowed down enough, your 4-year-old daughter could do James Earl Jones voiceovers. The Maintain Audio Pitch checkbox is to prevent the audio from changing pitch in proportion to the speed. The audio speeds up, but the pitch remains constant.

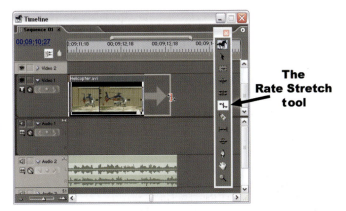

The Rate Stretch tool

Use the Rate Stretch tool in the same manner as the Trim tool to change a clip's speed.

Rendering

As fast and efficient as Adobe Premiere Pro is, you will reach a point when you will have to render at least a portion, if not most or even all, of your edited timeline.

Premiere Pro will display a red line above the areas where full frame rate can't be achieved on your system. Each system's power is different, but typically, complex sections, where there may be multiple layers of video and audio with effects and filters, need to be preprocessed or rendered to create a *preview clip*. The preview clip takes the place of the multiple clips and filters when you playback (without affecting the timeline) and eliminates any frame dropping you might experience in preview when you master out to tape. These rendered preview files are stored on your hard drive. When you render an area, the red line turns green. Any additional changes in that area may need rendering again.

The arrow shows the red line indicating that this area of the timeline will not play at full frame rate.

To set the area of the timeline you would like to render, use the Work Area bar. If the bar extends beyond the edges of your current timeline view, the easiest way to bring it into view is to double-click in the lower, darker area of the timeline ruler. This will bring the Work Area bar to the active Sequence window or the length of the sequence, whichever is shorter. To extend the Work Area bar to the correct length, you can drag the edges in much the same way as you can trim a clip on the timeline. The Work Area bar position can be moved by dragging on the textured area in the center of the bar, which many of us call the *tread*. You can also move the Work Area bar by hovering over any section of it and holding the Alt key; the cursor will turn into a hand, and you can drag the Work Area bar to a new position.

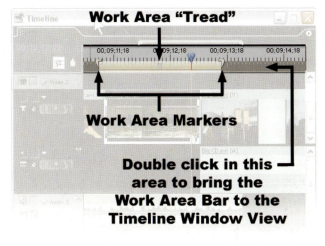

When the Work Area bar is the correct length and in the desired position, you can select Sequence ▶ Render Preview from the pulldown menu or simply press Enter. The part of the timeline bracketed by the Work Area bar will render. If you want to preview the timeline and save the rendering for later, simply press the spacebar.

Freeze Frame

To create a freeze frame so that an entire clip plays back frozen on one frame, do this:

1   Right-click on the clip you want to freeze in the timeline window.

2   Select Frame Hold in the context menu.

3   Click in the Frame Hold Options box and select whether you want the clip frozen at the In point, the Out point, or at Marker 0 (zero).

To place a Marker 0 on the clip, start with the clip in the Source window, position the cursor at the frame you wish to freeze, right-click in the Source window timeline, and select Set Clip Marker ▶ Next Available Numbered. If there are already other markers on the clip, you must reset Marker 0, because that is the only marker available for creating freeze frames.

Note: The way I like to do this is to go directly to Set Clip Marker ▶ Other Numbered. This will bring up a dialogue that will tell you the next numbered marker available. If it isn't zero, you can simply type in 0 to override the previous setting and move Marker 0 to your current position.

Also in the Frame Hold Options dialogue, the box marked "Hold Filters" should be checked if you have any filters changing settings over time that you want to freeze with the video.

The box marked Deinterlace should be checked if you have content with very fast action that shows saw-toothed edges on moving objects or excessive flickering when you freeze the frame.

EFFECTS

Premiere Pro has some very sophisticated effects capabilities. Effects for video and audio can be customized, combined, and changed over time. This chapter covers the basics to get you started working with transitions and effects.

To work with effects in Premiere Pro, you will need to work with the Effects window and the Effect Controls window. For purposes of screen space, I like to nest the Effects window in the Project window. The Effect Controls window can be nested in the Project window or the Source Monitor window. I prefer it in the Project window, because you can get more horizontal space to work the timeline there than in the Source Monitor window.

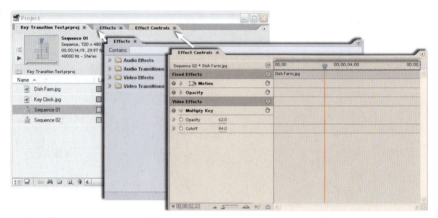

The Effects window and Effect Controls window can dock in the Project window.

The Effects Window

The Effects window is the storage area for effects and transitions. When you open it, you will see that it contains four folders, or *bins*:

- Audio Effects

- Audio Transitions

- Video Effects

- Video Transitions

The Effects window.

Inside each bin are nested bins to group the effects and transitions logically. To open a bin, click on the triangle to the left of the bin icon.

Use the effects and transitions in these folders by opening the appropriate folder and dragging the filter or transition to the timeline. The effects are dropped on a clip, and the transitions must be dropped on an edit point, or the in or out point of a clip. You may notice that we're dropping a cross dissolve transition on the in point of a title to fade it in. We could also place a transition on the in point of a clip to fade it up from black, etc.

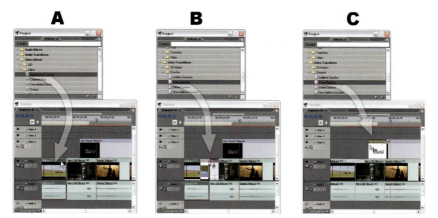

Three scenarios for dragging and dropping from the Effects window. A.) The Brightness and Contrast Filter is dragged directly to a clip. B.) A Cross Dissolve is dragged to a cut point as a transition. C.) A Cross Dissolve is dragged to the edge of a title clip with no adjoining shot, to be used as a fade-in.

You can create your own additional bins and drag frequently used effects into them. Create a new bin by clicking on the New Custom Bin button next to the

The New Custom Bin button.

garbage can at the bottom of the Effects window, or choose New Custom Bin from the Effects window menu. You can create one or several custom bins to organize your favorite transitions and effects. You can delete a custom bin by selecting it and clicking the Delete Custom Items button (the trash can) or by choosing Delete Custom Items from the Effects window menu.

The Effect Controls Window

The Effect Controls window is where you will customize how a filter or transition works over time.

The Effect Controls window when first opened. (You must have a clip on the timeline selected to see settings.)

When you open the Effect Controls window, you will notice that it isn't empty. Motion, Opacity, and Volume effects are built in, or *pre-applied,* to the clip and are immediately available for adjustment when you open the Effect Controls window. These are called *fixed effects.*

The Motion and Opacity Fixed Effects

The Motion effect allows you rotate, move, and scale your clip to create animated effects. The Opacity effect controls the transparency of a clip for fading a clip in or out and for some types of compositing. If the selected clip has audio, you will see the Volume control under Audio Effects.

There are three different ways to change the value of an attribute for most Premiere Pro effects and filters, including the Motion and Opacity effects in the Effect Controls window:

- Many settings have their own triangles, which will reveal a value slider.

- Or you can make a value adjustment by clicking and dragging over the hot text value to the right of the attribute.

- Or you can click the text value directly and type in a new value.

In addition to the adjustments available in the Effect Controls window, video

Twirl down triangle and drag the slider

Click and drag on hot text

The Show Keyframes button is indicated. Choose Show Opacity Handles to work with opacity settings on the timeline.

Click on the hot text and type in a value

clip opacity and audio clip volume can be adjusted on the timeline.

1 On the track you wish to adjust, click on the Show Keyframes button and select Show Opacity Handles.

2 Choose the Pen tool from the Tool palette.

3 To adjust the overall volume or opacity of the clip, click and drag the handle up or down as appropriate.

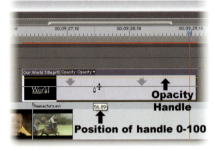

The Pen tool will automatically change to the Fade Adjustment tool when it's over the opacity handles.

To add keyframe adjustment points to the opacity or volume handles in the timeline, follow these steps:

1 With the Pen tool selected, hold the Ctrl key and click on the spot where the new keyframe will be.

2 Release the Ctrl key.

3 Now, click and drag the keyframe node to move it up/down or right/left as necessary.

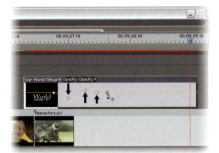

The Pen tool in the Tool palette.

4 Or click and drag any line segment up or down as necessary.

Hold the Ctrl key to create keyframes. Release the Ctrl key and the Pen tool will automatically switch between the Fade Adjustment tool, to move line segments, and the Keyframe Adjustment tool, to move keyframe points.

Note: You can move keyframe points with the Selection tool, but the Pen tool has more functionality overall to make opacity and volume handle adjustments.

The Motion effect also has alternate controls. When you click the small box with the arrow next to the Motion heading in the Effect Controls Window, you will see *nodes*, or handles, created around the corners and in the center of the

Program view. This can be helpful when the video frame you are moving must be placed with consideration for another layer of video. The picture-in-a-picture seen over a newscaster's shoulder is an example.

Click the box next to Motion in the Effect Controls window to send motion control to the Program view.

- Clicking and dragging the corner nodes will scale the video picture.

- Turning off Uniform Scale in the Effect Controls window will allow you to scale the frame nonproportionately.

- Moving the middle handle (the circle with the X inside) will reposition the entire frame.

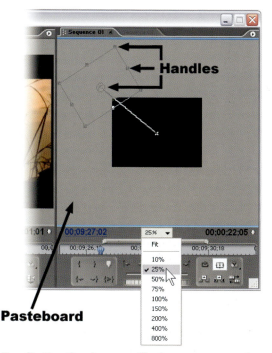

Pasteboard

By adjusting the view magnification, you can see the pasteboard area to aid in setting up motion in the Program view.

When adjusting Motion effects from the Sequence Monitor, it can be helpful to reduce the magnification in the monitor to view the area around the active video frame. This area is called the *pasteboard*, and it can be helpful to have it in view when you are moving clips on or off screen.

Applying Transitions

Video Transitions and Audio Transitions are available in the Effects window in specific bins. They are sorted into additional bins based on type and can be placed on any appropriate track (e.g., video transitions on video tracks, audio transitions on audio tracks).

To place a transition you'll need two clips with a cut between them on the same track in the timeline (and preferably some trimmed handles on each):

1 Open the Video Transition (or Audio Transition) bin by clicking on the triangle.

2 Select and drag the transition of your choice to the cut on the timeline.

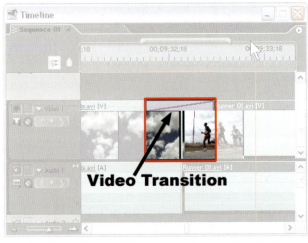

A placed transition will show up as a bar equal to the length of the transition on the top of the clip or clips.

Transitions can also be used on a clip if another clip to transition to is not available. For example, transitions can be used to make a title on a track above another clip appear and disappear.

There are three ways the transition can be placed:

• End at cut

• Center at cut

• Start at cut

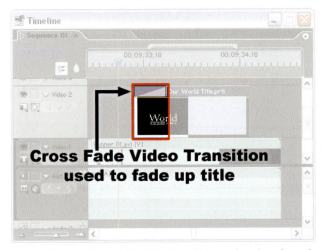

A transition can be used to fade in audio or video clips through placement along the leading or trailing edge of the clip.

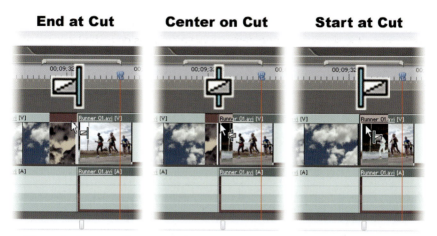

End at Cut   **Center on Cut**   **Start at Cut**

The symbol next to the cursor when you are dropping a transition will indicate whether you are dropping it to start, center, or end on the cut.

The available handles, or trimmed frames beyond the in and out points of the clips on the timeline, will affect whether or not all three placement choices are available to you. If there are no trimmed frames on the second clip (i.e., the in point on the timeline is the actual first frame of the raw clip), then the only option Premiere Pro will make available to you will be to start at the cut. Centering a transition on the cut can also be affected by insufficient handles. If there is very little handle on one clip and significantly more on the other, the Center at Cut option may not actually be centered, even though it will stretch out in both directions from the cut.

Creating a Default Transition

The preset default transitions are indicated by a red outline around the icons. The default video transition for video is the crossfade, and the default transition for audio is the constant power crossfade. These two transitions are probably the most frequently used by most editors. If you would prefer different default transitions, you can set them by taking these steps:

1   Select the transition you want to be the new default.

2   Choose Set Default Transition from the Transition palette menu.

3 Set the default transition's duration by choosing Default Transition Duration from the Effects palette menu.

4 The General Preferences dialogue will come up with separate choices for audio and video default durations.

Choose a transition from the menu and select Set Default Transition to set it. By selecting Default Transition Duration, you will open a Preferences dialogue, where you can enter a value.

To set the default transition at an edit point without dragging and dropping it, you can position the CTI on the cut you wish to transition, and you can place the default transition by using the keyboard shortcuts. The default keyboard shortcuts are Ctrl + D for the video transition and Ctrl + Shift + D for the audio transition. You can also select Apply Video Transition or Apply Audio Transition from the Sequence pulldown menu. Use the Page Up and Page Down keys to position the CTI directly on a cut point. Be sure to target the track where you want the transition.

Applying and Removing Effects

Effects are available in the Video Effects and Audio Effects bins inside the Effects window. You can drag Audio or Video effects directly from their bin onto the clip you wish to apply them to. You can also drag them directly into the Effect Controls window (as long as the Effect Controls window and the Effects window are not both nested in the Project window) when your clip is selected.

To delete an effect from a clip, open the Effect Controls Window and select the effect you want to remove in the list. From there, you can do one of these:

Click on the effect you want to remove and press Delete on the keyboard or right-click and select Cut from the context menu.

- Right-click on the effect and select Cut or Clear from the context menu.

- Choose Delete Selected Effect from the Effect Controls menu.

- Simply press Delete or Backspace.

Working with Keyframes

Each effect can be adjusted through dialogues available from the Effect Controls window, and attributes can be changed over time through *keyframing*. Each keyframe is a setting in time. Each effect or attribute will change state from keyframe to keyframe, changing over time.

Here's how to set a keyframe:

1   Find the attribute you would like to change over time and click on the small stopwatch symbol to the left of that setting or effect to enable keyframing.

2   Your first keyframe will automatically appear on the timeline where the CTI is parked.

3   Reposition the CTI and add additional keyframes by changing a setting or by clicking on the Add/Remove Keyframe button between the arrows.

Click on the stopwatch to enable keyframing.

Note: You might want to make a habit of placing the CTI at the beginning of the clip when you activate the stopwatch, to set the starting keyframe automatically.

4   Use the arrows on either side of the Add/Remove Keyframe button to jump between keyframes.

The Add/Remove Keyframe button.

Customizing Keyframes

Keyframes are not only a way to assign certain values to certain instances in time; they can also control the rate and concentration of the change that happens between those instances. For this, we need to utilize *keyframe interpolation*.

Each keyframe is capable of having two different interpolation attributes: an In and an Out. The In attributes affect how we arrive at the keyframe: whether we ease into it or hit it fast. The Out attributes control how we depart from it, or move forward from there: easing out or starting fast.

The shape of each keyframe has two parts that indicate how both the in and the out interpolations are set up. Starting and ending keyframes have only one

interpolation setting. Starting
keyframes will only have an Out
interpolation assignment, and
ending keyframes will only have an
In assignment.

There may be times when you want
to assign a keyframe value to a clip
outside of its trims. Perhaps you
want a type of motion that must
begin three frames before the shot's
in point to look exactly right. Or you
might want an audio clip to be
fading up from silence, but you want
to start the clip halfway through the
"ramp." To see beyond the trimmed
edges of your clip in the Effect
Controls window, access the
window's menu and make sure that
Pin to Clip is *not* selected. This will
allow you to scroll the timeline
display beyond the physical trims of
the clip on the timeline and create
keyframes outside of the trims.

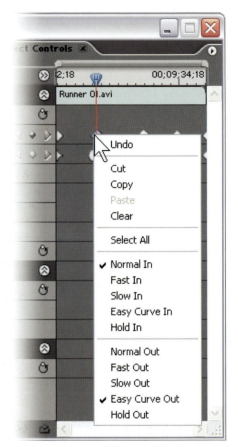

**Right-click on a keyframe to open the
keyframe context menu and change the
interpolation.**

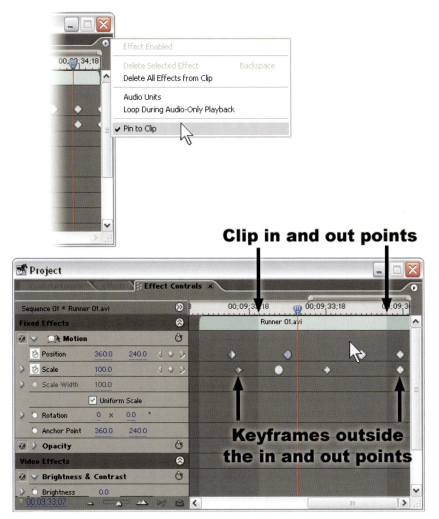

Clip in and out points

Keyframes outside the in and out points

Uncheck Pin to Clip in the Effect Controls window menu to place keyframes outside the in and out points of a clip.

ADOBE TITLE DESIGNER

As of version 6.5, the Adobe Title Designer replaced what had historically been a dependable, but basic, title tool. Anyone who has had any exposure to Premiere 6.5 or a later version through one of my seminars or tradeshow presentations knows this is one of my favorite parts of the software. Using it is fun and easy, and it comes with design templates that make creating professional-looking titles inside your Premiere Pro software faster than ever.

The first critical concept to understand is that the files created by the Title Designer are not somehow embedded in the project file. Although they will stay in your Project window like your other project media, they must be saved as separate files and used in your project like any other video, audio, or graphic clip. This also means that you can use them in more than one project if you wish.

My personal system is to save the Title Designer files inside the same folder as the rest of the media or graphics for any given project. That way all the components of a project can be found in one place and easily archived—or at least accessed by that replacement editor who has to come in and work on the project if I'm not available.

Creating a New Title Document

Choose File ▶ New ▶ Title to open Title Designer with a new, blank document. To do this from the keyboard, the default shortcut key is F9.

To save the title when you've composed it, select Save As from the File pulldown menu. Title Designer files save with the extension *.prtl*. You can open title files from v6.0 and earlier versions of Premiere, but Title Designer will immediately prompt you to resave it with a .prtl extension and update the file.

The default arrangement for composing in Title Designer is to open ready to create a *superimposed title*. This is a title that is transparent through to the video in the background, except for the foreground elements such as text and graphics. When the window opens, you will see whatever video frame your CTI is resting on in the background. If you do not want the video to show in the background, uncheck the Show Video checkbox above the composition area.

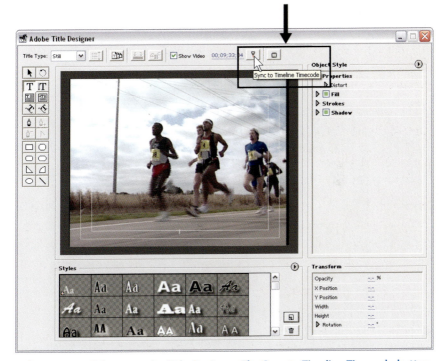

File ▶ New ▶ Title opens the Title Designer. The Sync to Timeline Timecode button will update the video background to display the current frame under the CTI.

Working with Text

Title Designer can be used to create a variety of text and graphic elements. Any vector font that is on your system, including True Type, Type 1, and Open Type, will work with Title Designer.

To type text into the window, follow these steps:

1   Choose either the Horizontal or the Vertical Type tool (the buttons with the letter T in the second row down along the left side of the composition area).

2   Click into the drawing area where the text should begin.

3   After you finish typing, click on the Select tool (the black arrow in the top row of tools), then click outside your new text object to deselect it.

Click on a Type tool, then click in the composition window and start typing.

To move or rearrange text objects, simply click and drag them with the Select tool. The Select tool can also be used to scale and rotate the text object. Vertical and horizontal scaling can be done by clicking and dragging the corner points (holding down Shift locks the aspect and scales each equally). The side points can scale either vertically *or* horizontally. The corner points can also be used to rotate the object by moving the cursor slightly outside the corner point, where it changes to a rotate icon.

Scale text objects by dragging the handles.

A titler is not a word processor, so it does not automatically "wrap" text at the end of a line when space runs out. Because we are arranging type visually, using the Enter key to wrap or to start a new line is the standard method with the Horizontal and Vertical Type tools. Adobe Title Designer does have a word wrap option, which you can turn on by choosing Title ▶ Word Wrap.

You can restrict the type to the predefined area of the text object box and have some automatic wrapping behavior by selecting the Horizontal Area Type tool or Vertical Area Type tool (just below the standard type tools). In the case of a text object created with the Area Type tools, scaling the text object will only affect the size of the text box. Unless you've typed in returns, the text will wrap to fill the new space.

An area type object can be resized with the object handles, but the text will redistribute itself into the new space rather than resize with the object.

Typing on a Path

The Path Type tools are located below the Area Type tools. Like the Type and Area Type tools, the Path Type tools are available in a horizontal or a vertical version. The Path Type tools allow you to form an irregular path in the form of a curve—or just about any path shape you can think of—and simply type in characters along that path.

To create type on a path, follow these steps:

1 Click on a Path Type tool.

2 The cursor will turn into a Pen tool; use it to draw a path, clicking to create points as you go.

3 When your path is complete, simply start typing.

Once the text is on the path, the text object itself can be resized using the object handles. Scaling with the object handles will scale the path. The text will remain the same size and redistribute itself along the path.

Create a path by clicking on points that form a path, then type in your text.

To resize the text, change the font size in the Object Style menu under the Properties heading, to the right of the Composition window. The text will redistribute itself to fit along the path.

To change the shape of the path, use the Pen tools (described in the next section) to move, add, or remove points on the path.

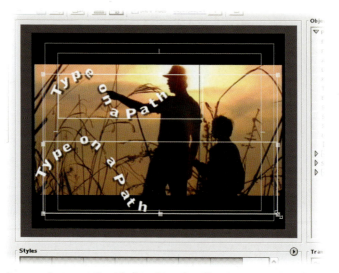

Resize a path text path with the object handles. You can resize the text itself only from Object Style menu.

Pen Tools

Directly below the Type tools, you will see the Pen tools. These tools can be used to draw lines in your composition. After your lines have been included in your composition, you can select any number of attributes for text, such as gradients, textures, and shadows.

To create a line or *path* object, do the following:

1   Select the Pen tool.

2   In your composition area, click several times, moving as you click to create a line.

3   When the line is drawn, you can click and drag the points along the path to change the route of the path and change the shape of the line object.

Once your graphic object is in your composition, you can right-click on it and use the Graphic Type menu to change the characteristics of the line object—or even change the line object to one of the shape choices.

After a path object has been created, right-click on it and select Graphic Type to select another graphic choice from the context menu.

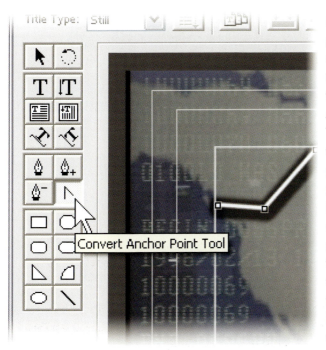

The Convert Anchor Point tool.

The tool that doesn't look like a pen, but more like a simple, upward-pointing arrow, is the Convert Anchor Point tool. This tool changes the behavior of a point from a simple point to a bezier (pronounced *bez-ee-ay*) adjustable point. *Bezier* refers to the type of curve tension adjustment that is available via handles created when you convert a simple point.

If you drag slightly (or even a lot) during each click when you are creating a path object, you will see the bezier handles appear and you will get a feel for the adjustment capability. Don't be afraid to experiment. Creating the bezier handles when you create the point will save you the step of using the Convert Anchor Point tool later.

By clicking and dragging when you are creating a point, you will create bezier handles for that point immediately, eliminating the need to convert the point later.

Working with Graphic Elements

You can also create shapes for building graphics from within the Title Designer. Several shapes are available in the lower section of the toolbox.

Here's how to create a shape in your title:

1 Select a shape from the toolbox by clicking on it.

2 Click and drag in the composition area to create the shape as a graphic element.

3 The shape can be dragged into position and scaled, as well as given text attributes, just like type.

Select a graphic shape and drag out a box in the frame to create a graphic element.

Your shapes can also be edited if you right-click on them and select Graphic Type ▶ Open (or Closed, or Filled) Bezier from the list. Use the Convert Anchor Point tool to create bezier handles on the shape's points, and adjust to your heart's content.

Note: You can make a title with a background that isn't transparent by dragging a rectangle the size of the frame and choosing a solid color, gradient, or texture for the rectangle. This creates an opaque background.

Object Styles

Along the right side of the composition window are the Object Style settings. Click on the triangle to the left of the word *Properties* to expand the menu.

The Object Style settings.

Before we go through the properties list, we need to create a text object. Follow the instructions for creating type to create a type object in the composition area.

Font

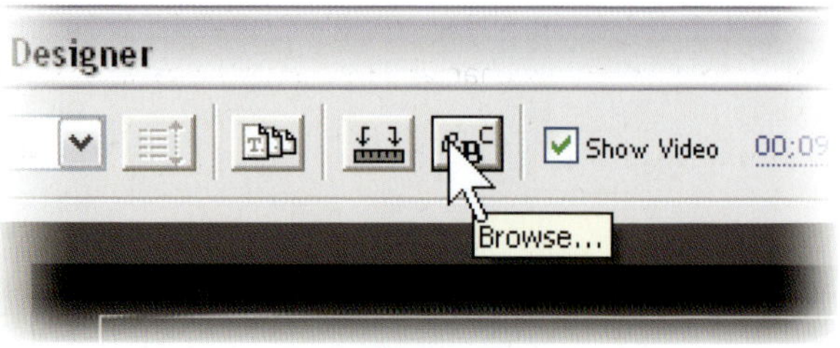

Starting at the top of the list, you will notice the font is listed. By clicking on the name of the font, you will call up a menu that

The Font Browse button.

includes the fonts on your system, so that you can choose and apply one to your text object. The only problem is that most of us have very little idea about the appearance of anything but the most familiar font names.

You can solve that problem by browsing the list visually:

1   Make sure you have a text object in the composition area and that it is selected.

2   Click on the Font Browse button above the composition area.

The Font Browser will open. Move it so you can see the type in your composition.

The Font Browser.

As you click or move the cursor down through different fonts, you will see your selected type object change font, while maintaining its other style attributes.

When you see a font that you like, simply click OK in the Font Browser.

Note: You can also reach the font listing by right-clicking on the type object and choosing Font ▶ Browse.

You can also access the Font Browser via a right-click on your text object and the context menu.

Font Size

No hidden meanings here—this is how you size your type. The size of the type is listed in scan lines. You can size a whole object if the object itself is selected. You can also size individual characters by dragging the I-beam over them and selecting them as you would in a word processor. Then you can alter the settings for those words or characters selected within an object.

Aspect

Aspect only sizes the type object or type horizontally. The setting value is telling you the percentage of the original width of the font you've selected.

Leading

Leading (pronounced *led-ing*) is the spacing between lines. Use leading when letters start to overlap with the line above or below and you want to add space.

Kerning

Kerning is the spacing between specific character pairs. There are times when the spacing between two letters just looks wrong. With fonts being created by so many people who may or may not be experienced typographers, kerning is almost a lost art these days.

To adjust kerning, you need a type object in the composition area. Then, follow these steps:

1   Select the Type tool.

2   Click between the two characters you want to adjust to make the flashing cursor appear there.

3   Click and drag on the kerning hot text adjustment to change the spacing between the two letters.

You can also kern an entire text object by selecting it and adjusting with the kerning hot text.

Adjust kerning by positioning the cursor and clicking and dragging over the hot text or by clicking on the hot text and typing a value.

Tracking

Tracking is like kerning, except that it is designed to work proportionately across an entire line of type. Tracking adjustment is based on the justification of the type. The character spacing will expand and contract from the justification point. Left-justified type will expand to the right, and center-justified text will expand from the center.

Baseline Shift

By shifting the baseline of your type, you can reposition it vertically in relationship to its adjacent characters.

The best way I know to demonstrate the utility of shifting type baselines is to make a price, like one might see in the North American television commercials, for which the dollars are large and the cents are smaller, but they are all semi–top justified:

1   Create a text object and type in a price such as $99.99.

2   Using the Type tool, drag-select the first *99* only, making sure that the rest of the text is not selected.

3   Use the Font Size setting to make those particular characters larger. The characters will remain bottom-justified, but we want them top-justified.

4   Keeping only those two characters selected, click on the hot text for Baseline Shift and drag to the right, until the position looks correct to you.

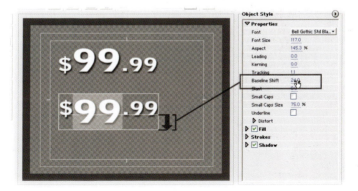

Use Baseline Shift with specific text selected to move characters vertically, separately from the rest of the text object.

Important note: After you have multiple settings for one attribute within a text object (as we just did for both Font Size and Baseline Shift), the hot text for that attribute will not display a number when the entire object is selected. If you use the hot text for an attribute with multiple settings, the entire text object will "snap" to one uniform setting, based on whatever adjustment you've made. You can adjust the size of the text object with the handles, however, while retaining all of your adjustments.

Slant

Think italics, adjusted by you in one-degree increments of tilt.

Small Caps

Small Caps converts lower-case letters to capital letters, with the value being the percentage of the size of the full-sized capital letters. You should enter a value for this attribute before checking the box; the default value setting is 1%, and if you don't realize this, your first experience with Small Caps will be microscopic!

Underline

Typical underlined text—not much explanation needed. This is not available for text on a path.

Distort

Distort offers another way to customize a look if you just can't find a font that's odd enough for your needs by itself. The X and Y values indicate the axis that you're distorting. This one is best experimented with to accommodate your personal taste.

Fill

The Fill settings adjust how you will present the main surface of your text. Fill is divided into three sections: Fill Type, Sheen, and Texture. Click on the arrow next to the word *Fill* to reveal the settings.

Fill Type

You have several choices you can access by clicking on the text field to the right of the words *Fill Type*. These range from Solid, which is simply a solid color, to a four-color gradient.

The eyedropper positioned below the Fill Type item can be used to pick colors from your video shot showing through in the composition window or from anything that is included in the interface. The eyedropper can pick colors for solids or gradients.

Sheen

Sheen refers to that glare you might see on something metallic and reflective. For sheen to work well, you should have a color chosen in the box that is significantly brighter than the Fill Type color(s). White or a very nonsaturated color works best for simulating metallic looks. Be aware that this setting defaults at a size value of zero, so you'll need to enter a value before you can see the effect. I'd recommend starting out with a value of 35 to see instantly what the effect does, then adjust from there.

An example of sheen used to give type a reflective, metallic look.

Texture

You can load a picture or graphic as a texture on your type or your graphic objects. Here's how:

1 Have a text object selected.

2 Click the Texture check box.

3 Click on the blank square to the right, which will open a Load dialogue.

4 Browse to the graphic you would like to load, then select it.

There are extensive adjustments available for rotation, scaling, blending, and tiling behaviors.

Strokes

If you're familiar with Photoshop's layer styles, these *strokes* are exactly the same thing. If you aren't a Photoshop user, the Strokes attribute is for creating outlines. Inner strokes happen inside the area taken up by the character; outer Strokes add mass to the character.

Shadow

Using shadows (also called *drop shadows*) has been a standard technique in video type for years. Shadows are useful for setting type off a background, making it more readable without having to outline. Shadows can also give the feel of some Z-axis depth to your video type.

The color is selectable; again, you'll notice the eyedropper. The Angle attribute controls where the light is coming from and therefore in what direction the shadow is falling. Distance controls how far offset the shadow is from the text. Size simply scales the shadow, and Spread controls how soft and diffused the shadow appears.

For a glow effect, try picking a very bright color for the shadow and cutting the Distance value to zero while increasing size and spread.

Transform

The Transform settings listing is useful for viewing the status of your object's position, rotation, and opacity. The hot text can be used to adjust these properties. You may notice that many of these controls are redundant, with controls elsewhere in the Title Designer window.

Type Styles

Below the composition area, you will notice a selection of text styles in the Style Swatch Display. You can apply these text styles to a text object by selecting the object and simply clicking on the swatch that represents the style you would like to apply. After you've applied the style, you can edit it with the Object Style settings.

Style swatches in the Style Library.

Saving Object Styles

After you've created an object style you're happy with, you may wish to save it for later use. (They're called *object styles* because you can apply them to any object, not just type.) To save an object style into the Style Swatch Display, click on the New Style button to the right of the Style Swatch Display, just above the trash can. A dialogue will open, giving you an opportunity to name the style. When you click OK, the style will appear as an additional swatch.

Style Libraries

Premiere Pro has several optional Style Libraries that are on your system and available to you. Go to the Style menu by clicking on the arrow in the upper left area of the Style Swatch Display, and select Load Style Library. Select the library you would like to load, and it will appear as additional swatches. If the load dialogue doesn't open to the proper directory, you should find your style libraries in C: ▶ Program Files Adobe ▶ Premiere Pro ▶ Presets ▶ Styles.

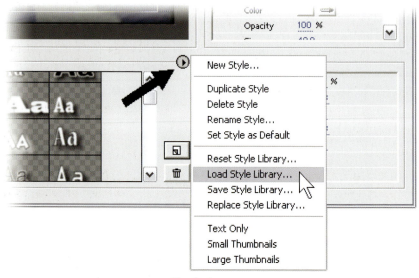

The Style menu.

It is possible to load all the Style Libraries at once. However, Premiere Pro remembers what you have in the Swatch Display and reloads the last settings when you open it. The more style swatches you have loaded, the longer it will take for the Title Designer window to open the next time.

To delete a style swatch, select it and click on the trash can or press the Delete key. Either way, you will be asked to confirm the deletion of the style.

You can save a Style Library of your own based on the swatches you have loaded. From the Style menu, select Save Style Library and name your library for later use.

Rolls and Crawls

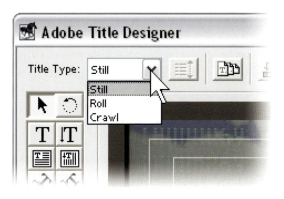

To create a *roll document*, as you might see used for credits at the end of a show, or a *crawl document*, as you might see scrolling across the bottom of a news channel screen, you must designate the proper choice for Title Type in the top left corner of the Title Designer window. This will default to Still. Click on the arrow and you can see the choices available.

Roll and crawl documents differ from a still document in that they allow you to type into an expanding window that can stretch out far beyond normal screen size. A roll will extend the text object vertically, and the crawl setting will expand horizontally.

The speed of the movement will depend on how long you stretch the clip on the timeline. If you place a Title Designer roll document on the timeline and make it 10 seconds, then you drag that exact same document to the timeline again and drag it out to 20 seconds, the text of the 20-second version will move half as fast as the other.

The button immediately to the right of the Title Type menu is the Roll/Crawl Options button. This will bring up a menu that has several choices for motion start and end and that gives you a choice of direction for crawls. You can choose to have a

Roll and crawl options.

roll or crawl start on-screen or off-screen and end on-screen or off-screen by checking the appropriate box. Preroll and Postroll refer to how long the file will wait to start moving the text and how long it will hold it at the end. We've all seen credit rolls that start with a very important bit of text, which is static for a time and then starts to roll. We've also all seen a credit roll stop and park for a while on the final credit. Ease-In and Ease-Out values will indicate how many frames you want the roll or crawl to use to accelerate to full speed and/or decelerate to a stop.

Working with Templates

Premiere Pro comes with a library of templates for you to use as inspiration and raw material for your title graphics. The button to access the templates dialogue is just to the right of the Roll/Crawl Options button. When the dialogue is open, click on the triangles to expand folders until you see files. You will notice that when you click once on a file, it previews for you in the window on the right side of the dialogue. This is very helpful for getting a visual idea of what you are loading. Checkerboard areas will look familiar to Photoshop users as *alpha transparent areas*, or areas where the video layer below shows through.

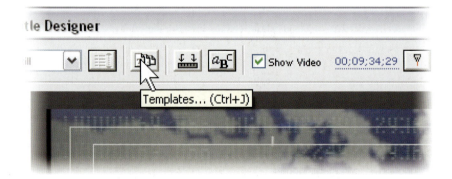

When you load a template, you will find that its components can be edited. You can drag, retype, change styles, and otherwise mold almost every setting and attribute available. If you want to save a document as a template for future use, click on the Templates button above the preview screen in the dialogue, then select Save (File Name) as Template.

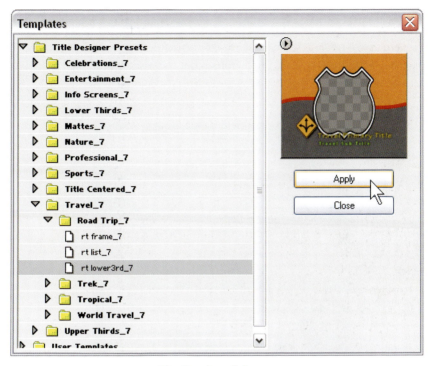

The Template dialogue.

You can select and change parts of a template.

Importing a Logo

There are several ways to load a logo or other graphic into Title Designer compositions. Most types of graphics from popular paint and drawing programs can be imported and given attributes, just as you would treat text.

Right-click in empty composition space and select Logo ▶ Insert Logo

Here's how to import a logo:

1   Right-click in the composition and choose Logo ▶ Insert Logo or go to the Title pulldown menu and choose Logo ▶ Insert Logo.

2   Select the graphic file you wish to load, which will be loaded at the size it was created.

3 You can now drag, size, and otherwise enhance the logo using the same tools you would use for text.

Previewing

You can preview to an external NTSC or PAL video monitor, if your system has one attached, by clicking on the Send Frame to External Monitor button.

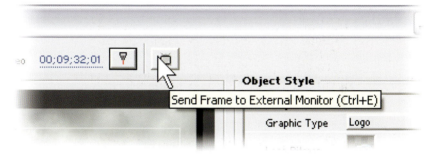

The Send Frame to External Monitor button.

If you have footage that is changing over time and you would like to visualize the title over several places on a clip, or even over several clips, you can drag the cursor over the hot text in the top of the Title Designer window to change the frame that is feeding through the background. You can also double-click directly on the hot text and type in the timecode numbers directly.

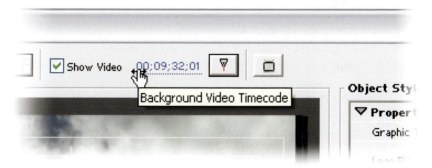

Use the hot text to change the frame from the timeline that is displayed behind your title.

WORKING WITH
AUDIO

Anyone who has worked with video editing on a computer knows that audio is an often overlooked part of the video editing process. Although audio capabilities are being reinforced in many video editing packages, Adobe Premiere Pro has brought audio capabilities for video editing to a new level.

Premiere Pro creates audio previews called *conformed* audio files. The complicated explanation of these files is that they're uncompressed 32-bit audio files created at the sampling rate defined in your project settings. The simple explanation is that they are very high-quality audio files, which allow Premiere Pro to preview audio effects very fast and efficiently at a high-quality level, but they can take up significant drive space.

Any audio that you bring into Premiere Pro—whether it's the sound that is part of a video clip, or a music bed or sound effect—must be conformed. Conforming takes place in the background and may affect your ability to use the clip while it's being done, and it may affect the speed of your system during the time conforming is happening. A short clip may conform without you realizing it's going on, but a long clip, such as an hour of DV material captured as one clip, could take some time. How much time this process takes depends on your system specifications.

The conformed audio files are created in the location you specify in Edit ▶ Preferences ▶ Scratch Disks ▶ Conformed Audio.

And, as you will see in this chapter, conformed audio is just the beginning of the changes and improvements for audio control in Premiere Pro.

Track-Based vs. Clip-Based Effects

The first general concept to understand is that you can affect audio in Premiere Pro in two ways: You can place effects and volume changes onto a clip, and a new feature in Premiere Pro is the ability to apply volume changes and effects to a track.

Applying level adjustments and effects to a clip results in level adjustments and keyframes that move with the clip if you choose to change its position. Effects and level adjustments made to a track will stay where they are, even if a clip is moved. In other words, if you had a clip that was very loud and you made a level adjustment to the audio track with the Audio Mixer to lower its level, then you decided to exchange that clip for a different one that was not too loud, the adjustment would be linked to the track and stay in place, most likely requiring you to readjust for the new clip.

Most experienced Non-Linear Video Editors are familiar with the concept of applying effects to audio clips. The new features and capabilities contained in the all-new Audio Mixer may make even the most seasoned editor seriously consider rethinking his or her workflow, moving the majority of audio work from the timeline to the Audio Mixer.

The All-New Audio Mixer

Experienced Premiere Pro users will notice the new Audio Mixer, a huge step forward from the audio mixers of Premiere's past versions. Users coming from another application may be surprised at the considerable power contained here. With features like automated mixing (deep down, what audio veteran doesn't really like flying faders?), submixes, full 5.1 surround, and Virtual Studio

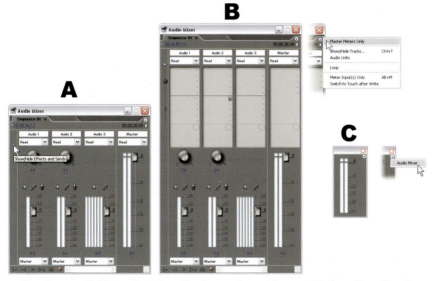

The three available Audio Mixer display modes. A. Open with the Effects/Sends hidden. B. Fully open. C. Master Meters only. Note the Audio Mixer menu choices to navigate between the views.

Technology (VST) plug-in support, experienced audio editors will definitely find some satisfaction with the audio processing power of Premiere Pro.

There are three choices for displaying the Audio Mixer. The Master Meters Only setting knocks the window down to a very small master levels display. With the Audio Mixer open, you have the option of showing or hiding the Effects/Sends area of the mixer.

Anyone new to video editing may find the Audio mixer a bit intimidating, but it is actually very efficient and logical. Even with the extensive capabilities in the mixer, the basic functions of the mixer are easy to understand.

The visual layout is familiar to audio pros who use mixing consoles. The familiar volume sliders work similarly to the volume sliders on a sound mixing board. In a way, changing the layout to vertical instead of horizontal makes the function of the sliders even easier to understand. Raising the slider increases the volume of that track in the mix, and lowering the slider decreases the volume of the track in the mix.

There are sliders for each mono, stereo, and surround channel in your timeline. There are also sliders for submixes and a slider for master volume. The master fader will always be on the far right side of the mixer. If you can't see all the tracks in the mixer, they may be outside the window's view. You can scroll left or right or increase the size of the window to bring missing tracks into view.

Beside each fader is the corresponding volume unit (VU) meter. The display in the VU meter gives a visual indication of the level of the sound on the track. The VU meters on the master and submix tracks show the level of the *summed*, or combined, audio tracks routed to them.

Audio levels can create an endless discussion with diverse opinions, particularly when it comes to analog vs. digital levels. Analog audio has always been referred to as having *headroom* (or ability to handle excess audio level) above 0 dB, but digital has no headroom at all.

When you're working in Premiere Pro using DV or another digital video format, the basic idea is that 0 dB is as far as you can go. The numbers indicating the values are beside the volume fader. With digital audio, exceeding 0 dB will result in *clipping,* which simply cuts off any data exceeding 0 dB, causing potentially severe audio defects or *artifacts.* Keep in mind that although individual tracks may all be within acceptable limits, after they've been combined, the sound level from the summed tracks may be too high. Decrease the master volume fader or the individual track faders as necessary to make sure that your levels are within acceptable range.

Channel Panning

In sequences where the master out is stereo or mono, you will see a pan knob above the slider on mono and stereo tracks to pan the channel from stereo left to right. If the master output for the sequence is 5.1 surround, you will see the 5.1 Surround Pan/Balance tray on each mono and stereo channel. These controls are to slide the audio "presence" from channel to channel, giving the viewer the perception of spatial movement or presence. The power of surround sound is well known. We've all been in a theater and been affected by a savvy sound mixer. Our eyes tell us that the objects we see are in two dimensions—while our ears make a convincing argument for three.

Stereo Sequence

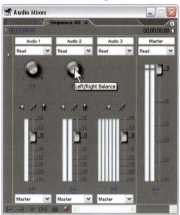

Surround 5.1 Sequence

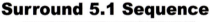

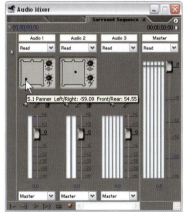

The Audio Mixer from a stereo sequence and from a 5.1 surround sequence. Note the Pan/Balance trays on the surround project.

There are three symbols above the faders. They are the Mute Track button, the Solo Track button, and the Enable Track for Recording button.

Mute Track: (Speaker icon). Use this to exclude a track from playback to focus on mixing other tracks or to compare different mixes.

Solo Track: (Trumpet icon). Use this when you need to concentrate on just one track. Another definition for Solo could be "Mute everything but this track."

Enable Track for Recording: (Microphone icon). Use this control to enable recording directly to the timeline. Use this setting and a microphone plugged into your computer to do voiceovers directly to the timeline.

Automating Changes in the Audio Mixer

You can set the Audio Mixer to record your adjustments as you make them, when making audio-level adjustments using the faders or channel adjustments using the panpots or the Surround tray during playback.

To adjust the level or pan as the program plays back:

1 Position the CTI at the point on the timeline where you want to start your changes.

2 Select Write from the pop-up menu above the channel(s) you want to affect on the Audio Mixer.

3 Click the Play button in the Audio Mixer window.

4 Make changes on the control surface of the Audio Mixer for levels or panning.

5 After you've finished the changes, reset the pop-up(s) to Read.

6 Position the CTI to a point before your changes and click the Play button once more to play back your changes.

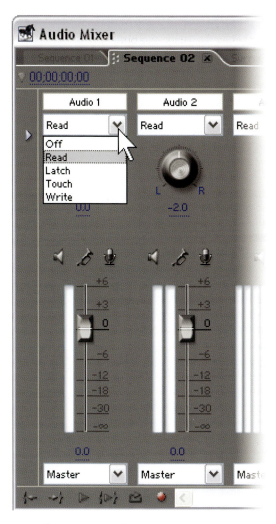

The automation choices are located in the pop-up just above the channel controls.

There are several different record and playback modes available on the Audio Mixer.

Off

This setting completely ignores your settings for the track during playback. Use this setting when you want to disable a previous mix and have manual control of the mixer.

Read

This mode tells the Audio Mixer to read all your stored settings during playback of the track. All your effects and level adjustments will be heard during playback. If you attempt to change a setting during playback on a track with Read selected, the control will simply snap back to its original location as soon as you let go of it, and no changes will be recorded.

Write

Unless you have a track control set to Safe During Write, this mode will record the adjustments you make. Each adjustment will create keyframes in the timeline as you play the program and operate the controls. Write mode creates keyframes as soon as you begin playback. Even if you only play back a track in Write mode and make no adjustments, you will have created keyframes.

Latch

Similar to Write mode. The difference is that you don't actually create a keyframe until you make a change. The control stays in the position in which you left it after adjustment.

Touch

Similar to Latch mode. The difference is that after you make the adjustment and release the fader, the fader will return to the value it started with, as opposed to staying in the position in which you left it (for information about setting Automatch Time, see page 11).

Note: You can choose to make a track Safe During Write. You can select this option by right-clicking on an effect or on the panpot or fader for each channel. This will lock the chosen settings (chosen effect, pan, or level) for all tracks while you are using Write, Latch, or Touch mode to record other mixing commands. Use this in cases where, for example, you've set up your mix but now want to work with stereo or 5.1 channel panning only. Choosing Safe During Write for the volume faders will prevent you from accidentally moving one while you're working with your panpots.

Applying an Effect to a Track

There may be times when you need to apply an effect to an entire track. For example, if you have footage from multiple shoot setups, and one location had a noise that needs to be filtered with an equalizer, you may want to dedicate one track to only those clips and set the proper effect once. That way the effect is consistent, and you don't have to set the effect for each separate clip individually. An effect is set for a track from the Audio Mixer.

First of all, verify that you have the Audio Mixer fully open. There should be large blank areas above the panpots for each channel. These are the areas where we'll set up our effects.

Effects Area

Sends Area

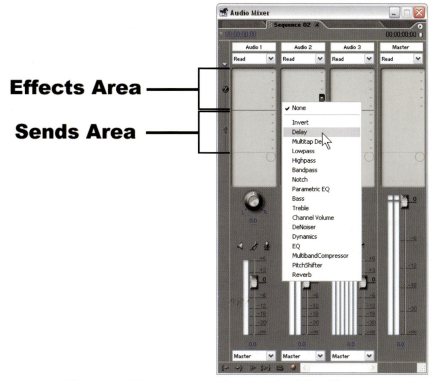

Click on one of the arrows along the right side of the Effects area
to open the Effects menu.

You will notice that these areas seem to be broken into sections. The top section is for selecting effects. Each channel has the capacity for five separate effects. If you run your mouse down the top area, you will notice that each area highlights as you roll over it. On the right side of each effect slot is an arrow. Clicking this arrow will open a menu of the effects available to Premiere Pro. Select an effect from this menu, and you will see it take a position in your selected place on the Effects list for that channel or track.

Some effects, such as a simple Delay, will have only a knob at the bottom of the Effects space to make simple adjustments. Other, more sophisticated effects, like the MultibandCompressor, will have their own control panels, which open when you double-click on their name in the Effects list.

Here, a Delay effect has been added to channel 2 in the Audio Mixer. The knob at the bottom of the Effects/Sends area adjusts its value.

To apply an effect to a track, do the following:

1   Place an audio clip or group of audio clips on Audio 1 (a human voice would be very good to use for this demonstration).

2   On the Audio Mixer, go to the to Audio 1 and click on an arrow on the right side of Audio 1's Effects area to open the Effects menu.

3   Select Reverb from the bottom of the menu.

4   Click and drag up on the knob at the bottom of the Effects area to increase the intensity of the effect (you should see the knob rotate and the setting change). Or you can right-click on the name of the effect and select Edit from the menu list to access the full controls for this effect.

5   Play your clip on the timeline.

The Effects Bypass button.

To temporarily disable an effect to listen to your audio without it, click on the small Bypass button (cleverly disguised as an ornate "f") at the bottom of the Effects area.

Along the bottom of the Audio Mixer window, you will notice transport controls. When you are working with the Audio Mixer, these controls control playback of the timeline, just as the Program View controls do. Use these controls to preview audio effects by applying the effect and using the transport controls to play the track.

If there is an area you know you'll be working with in detail, place an in point and an out point on the timeline and use the Loop setting at the bottom of the Audio Mixer to loop that section continuously as you make adjustments.

To remove an effect from a track, return to the Effects menu for the effect you wish to remove and select None.

There are instances when the results from an effect can change significantly, depending on whether the effect was applied before or after the volume control was applied, particularly when a large volume adjustment was necessary. By right-clicking on the name of the effect, you can choose Pre-Fader to apply the effect before the volume adjustments or Post-Fader to apply the effect after the volume has been adjusted.

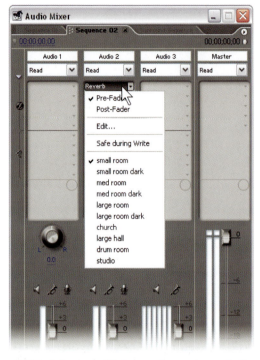

Right-click on an effect name to open a context menu that will give you Pre-Fader and Post-Fader options and (in this case for the Reverb effect) a selection of presets.

Submixes

In the days when all these audio effects could only be achieved through the use of expensive analog equipment in a large rack, unlimited channels of things like reverb, delay, and compression just weren't possible because of the expense. There were times when one channel of a particular effect was all a studio had, even though that effect was needed on multiple channels. To achieve the effect without a separate recording pass to process each channel separately, the studio needed to do a *submix*. The submix would combine all the channels that had to go through the effects device so that the device would only have to process the audio once, but the channels would be mixed properly so that their relative volumes were correct going into the final mix.

Why would you need to do a submix in Premiere Pro when you have all these channels available to you? The answer has less to do with your options than with your processing power. If you apply an effect to three channels separately, each with its own version of reverb, for example, Premiere Pro must apply that effect three different times, treating it as if it were actually three different effects. Use a submix to mix those three channels together *before* applying the reverb effect once to the submix, and you effectively use only a third of the resources to do it.

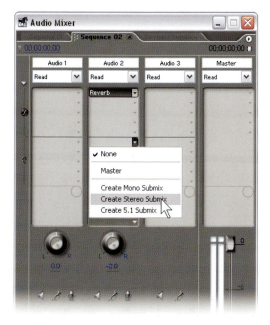

There are also times when effects will simply interfere with each other if applied to different files. Three tracks of audio playing back with three different reverb applications just won't sound the same as having the tracks mixed before the effect. A consistent effect across all three tracks creates a more realistic sound.

Click on a triangle along the right side of the Sends area to open the Submix menu.

The area above the panpots, where we've focused for our effects work, is called the Effects/Sends area. We need to *send* a channel or track to a submix. The Sends area is below the Effects area. If you click on an arrow along the right side of the lower half of this area, you will notice that the menu that comes up has to do with creating submixes.

To create a submix, follow these steps:

1   Click on an arrow on the right side of the column to open the Send menu.

2   Select Create Stereo Submix (or Mono or 5.1, depending on your needs).

3   A new channel will appear in the Audio Mixer, and a new track will appear in the timeline, representing your submix.

4   The track from which you created the submix is already routed through that submix. To route another track to the submix, click on an arrow in the Sends area of another track, and select the submix from the menu.

5   Apply effects to the submix as you would to any other track in the Audio Mixer.

The relative volumes of the tracks in the submix are controlled by the volume slider on the individual tracks. It's possible to send a track to a combination of submixes and the master track by selecting more than one send in the Sends area. A volume knob, indicating the volume level being sent to each destination, will appear at the bottom of the Effects/Sends area as each destination is selected.

You can route any track to any submix. Keep in mind that the type of audio that finally goes to tape will depend on the master settings for your sequence. You can have mono, stereo, or 5.1 channel surround sound tracks or submixes all included in the same sequence, but you can only output to stereo if that is your sequence's master setting.

Track Display in the Timeline Window

As many controls as you have available in the Audio Mixer, there are even more available in the timeline itself. In the area where you find the name of the track on the far left side of the Timeline window, there are several controls that affect how we view the timeline.

Use the adjustment knob at the bottom of the submix area to adjust the level or the channel balance going to the submix, depending on your selection in the pop-up menu just below the knob.

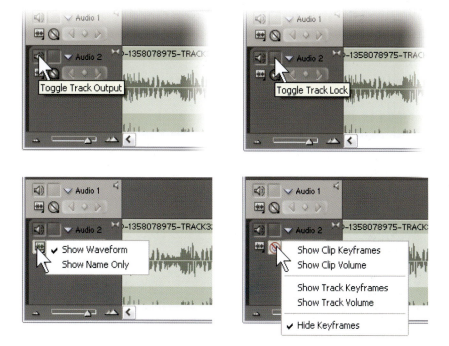

Keyframe navigation and Add/Remove Keyframe button

Each audio track in the timeline has several display options and keyframing controls.

Toggle Track Output

This "speaker" button can turn the track on and off. There will be times when you are working with multiple audio tracks and you need to silence one or several of them to concentrate on the adjustment of another.

Toggle Track Lock

This button, to the right of the Toggle Track Output button, can protect a track from unintended changes. Click on this button to make the padlock appear, and the track's attributes will be locked, including clip position, clip attributes, and track attributes. This will also lock out any unintended changes from happening on this track in the Audio Mixer.

Collapse/Expand Track

This triangle, just to the right of the Toggle Track Lock button, reveals the area where audio waveforms and the volume handles can be displayed. The track must be expanded for you to view the other buttons on this list. After the track has been expanded, you may want to adjust the track height by dragging the bottom edge of the track to make the working area larger.

Set Display Style

This button is only visible when the track is expanded and will produce a menu that gives you the option of showing the audio waveform or the name of the clip only. The audio waveform is very useful to view when you are editing audio, but it may slow the display down a bit on a slower system.

Show Keyframes

The Show Keyframes button is just to the right of the Display Style button and will open a menu with several options. Show Clip Keyframes will display any keyframes you might have associated with a clip-based audio effect. These keyframes would be the same ones created in, and visible in, the Effect Controls window. Show Clip Volume will turn on the volume handles, or *rubberbands* as some seasoned Premiere users may refer to them. Any keyframes you have created with the volume handles will also be visible. Show Track Keyframes and Show Track Volume work the same way as the Clip settings, but these will show you the volume and keyframe information that you have generated with the Audio Mixer. Hide Keyframes turns off all this information entirely.

Keyframe Navigation Tools

Directly under the track name (when the track is expanded) are the Keyframe Navigation tools. They work exactly like the Keyframe Navigation tools in the Effect Controls window. The arrows will move you forward or back to the next or previous keyframe, and the middle button is used to add or delete keyframes.

Adjusting Clip Audio Levels

There are times when a particular clip needs individual volume adjustment. The volume level of a clip can be adjusted in the Timeline window. Unlike the adjustments made in the Audio Mixer, the volume adjustments you make to the clip itself in the Timeline window will move with the clip when it is repositioned.

The clip volume handles can be adjusted using the Pen tool.

To adjust the audio levels of a clip, follow these steps:

1 Next to the name of the track on the left side of the Timeline window, click on the triangle for Expand/Collapse Tracks to expand the track if it isn't currently expanded.

2 Select the button to the right of the Display Style button and choose Show Clip Volume from the menu.

3 Click on the Pen tool in the Tool palette.

4 Use the Pen tool to move the audio volume handle up and down across the entire length of the clip when the Pen tool changes to the Fade Adjustment tool.

5 You can create keyframes to vary the level along the clip by Control-clicking along the line segment to create clip volume keyframes.

6 Keyframes can be moved with the Pen tool or the Select tool once they are created.

Note: The Pen tool will automatically change state as you move over keyframe nodes and line segments, allowing you to adjust either without changing tools.

Note: Each keyframe's interpolation can be set, just as it can inside the Effect Controls window, by right-clicking on a keyframe and selecting the interpolation setting(s).

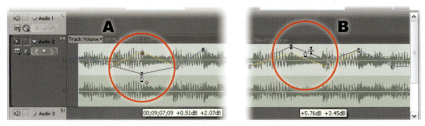

The Pen tool moves (A) keyframe nodes or (B) line segments, based on where you position your cursor.

Applying a Clip Audio Effect

The Audio Effects folder has effects grouped by audio type.

Applying audio effects to individual clips, as opposed to entire tracks, can be done on the timeline. Audio effects are categorized in the Audio Effects folder by the type of audio they are designed to handle. The Mono, Stereo, and 5.1 folders each contain the same list of effects, but make sure that you are choosing from the appropriate folder for the type of audio to which you are applying the effect.

Here's how to apply an effect to an audio clip:

1   Place an audio clip on the timeline.

2   In the Effects window, open the Audio Effects folder.

3   Open the appropriate folder inside, based on the type of audio clip you've chosen.

4   Drag the effect to the timeline and release it over your chosen clip.

Each audio effect has a different amount of adjustment available through the Effect Controls window. Although each effect is structured differently, the access to the adjustments works the same. Let's try one effect to demonstrate how this works.

1   Place a clip with audio on the timeline (a human voice would be a good clip to use for this effect).

2   Open the Audio Effects folder in the Effects window and open the appropriate folder: Mono, Stereo, or 5.1.

3   Select PitchShifter from the list and drag it onto your clip. Or, if the clip is selected and the Effect Controls window is open, you can drag the effect into the Effect Controls window.

4   In the Effect Controls window, you will see PitchShifter in the Audio Effects list. Use the triangle to the left of the name to open the settings, then click the triangle next to Custom Setup to see the adjustments for this effect.

5   By clicking and dragging over the knob on the left labeled Pitch, you will adjust the pitch of your audio.

6   Use the spacebar to play back your changes. By using the Bypass check box above the adjustment knobs to temporarily disable the effect, you can compare the sound with and without the effect.

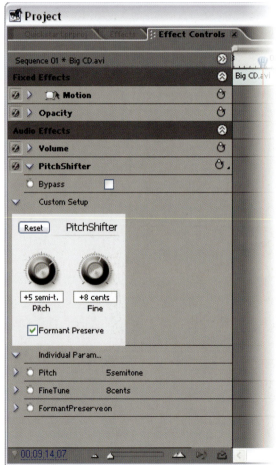

As you can see, the PitchShifter has more adjustments than just this one control. Each effect's custom controls will be different and appropriate to that effect's operation. Readers who are familiar with audio processing will

The PitchShifter effect adjustments in the Effect Controls window.

find the naming conventions to be fairly self-explanatory. For those who are just becoming familiar with audio effects, the online help has explanations of the functions of different effects; experimentation will help as well.

Fading and Crossfading

In many video editing software packages, the primary method of fading or crossfading audio is stacking the two audio clips on two different audio tracks with some overlap, then using the volume handles, or something similar, to simply ramp one in from silence as you ramp the other one out to silence, using the volume handles.

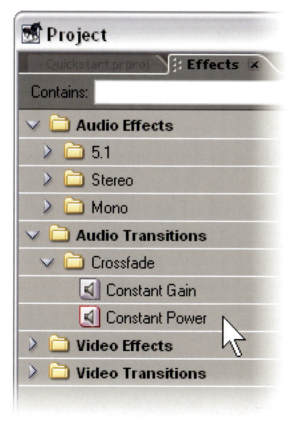

The Constant Gain and Constant Power audio transitions.

Premiere Pro has made this process far easier and faster by allowing the use of audio transitions, which are used exactly like video transitions. They can be used on cuts in line on a single track, or they can be used on the in or out point of a clip to fade it in or out, with no adjacent clip on the same track. The two options for audio crossfade are Constant Gain and Constant Power. Constant Power will produce a fade that sounds very linear or smooth to the ear, but may not actually be a flat ramp, mathematically speaking. Constant Gain will produce a smooth, technically flat ramp up or down, but it may not sound that way to the ear.

To apply an audio transition to fade audio, do the following:

1   Place an audio clip on the timeline.

2   In the Effects window, open the Audio Transitions folder.

3   Open the Crossfade folder and pick one of the crossfade transitions.

4   Drag the transition to the timeline, and release it on a cut or on the in point or out point of the clip.

5   Use the Select tool, which converts to the Trim tool along the edge of the transition, to adjust the length of your transition.

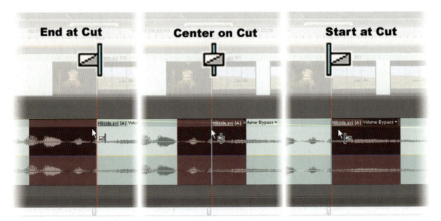

Apply an audio transition as you would a video transition.

To apply your default audio transition, position your CTI on a cut or the edge of a clip and press Ctrl + Shift + D.

The starting length of your transition when you apply it, called the *default* length, can be changed. Go to the pulldown menu Edit ▶ Preferences ▶ General and alter the default length in seconds or fractions of a second.

CONTENT AND PROGRAM OUTPUT

Video editing today is a much different process from what it was even seven to ten years ago. One area of video editing that has changed considerably is the options for outputting our programs. Even during the early to mid-1990s, when video editing was migrating from rooms full of video tape decks and other extremely expensive equipment to somewhat less costly desktop computers, the goal for output of the program was almost always the same videotape or film stock on which programs had been distributed for years.

Today the options for program distribution are expanding, due to a seemingly endless variety of compression options and distribution media. Users are editing programs for distribution on film, tape, CD-ROM, DVD, computer hard drives, flash RAM, video games, and the Internet. Premiere Pro has a very capable toolset for getting your program out of your machine and into the hands of your viewers.

Preparing a Program for Mastering

Depending on the ultimate destination for your program, you may want to prepare your program differently. For television commercials and programs that will be distributed on videotape, it is always best to put a test pattern (*bars and tone*) on the beginning of the tape. The test pattern, the universal language of all the equipment that will handle or process your video, helps broadcast or duplication technicians handle your program properly. Check with the television station or duplication facility for specific requirements for master tapes, such as test pattern length, audio tone level, black needed before program start, and whether or not a countdown or leader is required.

Common practice for a duplication master might be as follows:

- 60 seconds of bars and tone

- 10 seconds of black

- 10 seconds of slate (a simple title identifying what the program is and who you are, in case there are concerns or questions about the master)

- 10 seconds of black before program begins (Alternately, some television stations may still request a 10-second countdown.)

Some broadcast network submission requirements ask for program start to be at an exact timecode. Many editors will start bars and tone in the timeline at 00:58:00:00, so the program will always start two minutes later at exactly one hour (01:00:00:00). However, some consumer DV devices always start recording at 00:00:00:00 and don't allow you to set a different value manually. Unless you're supplying your DV footage to a television network, setting a specific timecode probably won't present a problem.

Here's how to create a Bars and Tone clip in your project:

1 From the File pulldown menu, select New ▶ Bars and Tone.

2 The Bars and Tone clip will appear in the Project window.

3 Drag the clip into your timeline.

Adobe Premiere Pro		
File Edit Project Clip Sequence Marker Title Window Help		

New ▶	Project	Ctrl+N
Open Project... Ctrl+O	Sequence...	
Open Recent Project ▶	Bin	Ctrl+/
Close Ctrl+W	Offline File...	
Save Ctrl+S	Title...	F9
Save As... Ctrl+Shift+S	Bars and Tone	
Save a Copy... Ctrl+Alt+S	Black Video	
Revert	Color Matte...	
Capture... F5	Universal Counting Leader...	
Batch Capture... F6		
Import... Ctrl+I		
Import Recent File ▶		
Export ▶		
Get Properties for ▶		
Interpret Footage...		
Timecode...		
Exit Ctrl+Q		

Note: If your program starts at the very beginning of your timeline, you may have to push your program material down the timeline to allow for the Bars and Tone clip and whatever else is required before program start. To accomplish this, you can use the Track Select tool with the Shift key to shift all tracks down the timeline, or you can perform insert edits at the beginning of the timeline.

You can create a countdown leader by selecting File ▶ New ▶ Universal Counting Leader.

If you are planning to output to an MPEG, QuickTime, or Windows Media file, or some other file format designed to be viewed on a computer screen, a test pattern will most likely be neither necessary nor desirable.

Export to Tape

The tape remains, for now, a likely destination for your program. If you are using a standard FireWire connection (also called iLink and IEEE-1394) and a DV camcorder or video deck, the connections are fairly straightforward. One FireWire cable will carry both audio and video to your camcorder or deck, just as it probably used the cable to bring in the footage and sound from that deck.

Note: If you are exporting your program to DV tape via FireWire, be sure to open your DV Playback Settings dialogue (from the Monitor window menu). Verify that Play Audio on DV Hardware is selected under the Export To Tape settings.

The DV Playback Settings dialogue.

If you have a video card that can record and/or capture analog video and audio, you might have to connect more than one cable. If you are making all or a part of your living with Premiere Pro, you may want to get an analog (usually RS-422) deck control plug-in so that Premiere Pro can connect to and control decks other than DV. Deck control allows you to place the program more precisely on the tape, particularly if you need to edit something and insert a section into an existing master tape.

By selecting File ▶ Export ▶ Export to Tape, you will open the Export to Tape dialogue.

The Export to Tape dialogue.

Under Device Control, you will see several check boxes:

Activate Recording Device: Check this box to get remote control of your video deck. If you need to take an existing program and add it to the end of your tape at a particular point, you will need this box selected so that Premiere Pro can control the edit point.

Note: It is best to "black" any DV tapes by recording the entire length of the tape with your camcorder's lens cap on before recording material on the tape from Premiere Pro. This will produce continuous timecode for the length of your tape, ensuring that Premiere Pro will always be able to navigate to the proper timecode location. If the program is destined for broadcast and your recorder allows you to set timecode, you may want to start with 00:58:00:00, as discussed earlier.

Assemble at timecode: Check this box and enter the timecode from your tape where you want to start recording new material.

Delay movie start by _____ quarter frames: Some DV video decks can experience a slight delay between detecting the proper position to edit "in" and actually beginning recording when the tape is playing back. You may want to experiment with your deck to determine how much, if any, delay is necessary to synchronize your deck with Premiere Pro.

Preroll: As in the ancient days of the early 1990s, when deck-to-deck video editing was state-of-the-art technology, video decks need to back up and use some *preroll* to get up to speed and to synchronize with the other devices involved with the edit. Many decks will be fine with 150 frames (5 seconds) of preroll.

Under Options, there are additional check boxes:

Abort after _____ dropped frames: Check this box to stop the export if a certain number of dropped frames is detected. Type the number of dropped frames you want to have trigger an abort. I usually leave this on, because dropped frames usually aren't acceptable under any circumstances for our projects. I would rather have the export stop, so that I can fix the problem and not waste time exporting the entire program just to repeat the process.

Report dropped frames: Check this box to have Premiere Pro track the frames that have been dropped during an export. I also always keep this one on, although when I ask it to stop on a dropped frame, it only counts to 1.

Render audio before export: Check this box to render audio effects and transitions before performing the export if you have a complex audio track that may prevent real-time export. Audio rendering is usually not nearly as time-consuming as video rendering, so I usually render the audio as a matter of practice before export.

The Export Status area displays any dropped frames that may have accumulated, the status of your record device, and the starting, ending, and current timecodes.

Once your settings are complete, select the Record button to export or the Cancel button at the bottom of the dialogue to exit. (Note that if the Cancel button is selected, the settings will be lost.)

Manual Recording

If you are exporting your program to a video recorder through some other means than FireWire and you do not have direct control of the deck, you will have to operate both the computer and your deck manually.

To record your program to a video deck manually, follow these steps:

1 Open the project and sequence you want to export.

2 Play the sequence back and monitor the input of your deck to verify that the audio and video are coming through to your deck.

3 Position the tape at the point where you wish to start recording.

4 Position your CTI a second or two before the beginning of your program (or test pattern).

5 Start your deck recording, then click on the Play button in the Program Monitor or press the spacebar to start playback.

6 When the program is finished, click on the Stop button in the Monitor window or press the spacebar again before stopping the recorder.

Export to DVD

A new feature with Premiere Pro is the Export to DVD option. With a compatible DVD burner connected to your system, this option will allow you to create an *autoplay* DVD. This type of DVD will automatically start to play when inserted in a DVD player. This option does not allow you to use menus, as you could by using a DVD-authoring program like Adobe Encore DVD, but you can use your timeline markers as chapter points to allow a DVD player to skip to various key points in the program.

Important note: Premiere Pro needs enough space to create your DVD on your hard drive before physically burning the DVD. Make sure there is sufficient space on your hard drive to create the scratch files for your export while still preserving scratch space for other tasks.

To export a sequence to DVD:

1 Have your project and sequence open. If you don't want to export your entire sequence, you can create a work area to define a section of the sequence.

2 From the pulldown menu, select File ► Export ► Export to DVD.

3 The Export to DVD dialogue will open.

4 Set up your settings as needed (specifics to follow).

5 Insert a compatible blank DVD in your DVD burner.

6 Click on Record to begin.

In Export to DVD, you will be specifying the following settings.

Under General panel:

• You can accept the default name that Premiere Pro picks based on the current date and time, or you can select Custom from the Disc Name pop-up menu and type in the disc name.

The General panel in the Export to DVD dialogue.

- Check the box for Loop Playback if you want the program to repeat automatically.

- Check the box for Chapter Points at Timeline Markers to create chapter points at each timeline marker in your sequence.

Under the Encoding panel:

- You can choose a preset from the Preset pop-up menu or a custom setting by selecting Custom Preset or New. (If you aren't familiar with the technical aspects of DVD production, the preset settings are designed to be compliant with the widest variety of DVD players.)

- In the Export Range pop-up menu, you have the choice of exporting your entire sequence or restricting the export to the Work Area.

- The Fields pop-up menu allows you to choose the field dominance of your material. DV source material should be set to Lower; if your source material is progressive scan, choose None.

- Check the box next to Maximize Bitrate if you want Premiere Pro to override the preset settings and use the maximum bitrate that is allowed by the space available on your DVD. (This may result in a file that falls outside of DVD specifications.)

**The Encoding panel in the Export to DVD dialogue
with encoding presets pop-up menu.**

- If Maximize Bitrate is checked, you will notice that you have the option to force variable bitrate, based on the content.

Bitrate is another one of those little items that could tack a chapter onto this book—or maybe a book onto this book.

Compression in general is a mysterious art. It's not a question of what *is* best so much as what *looks* best. Because our eyes rarely tell us the whole truth anyway, video compression schemes can throw out huge amounts of one thing keeping something else to fool the eye into believing it sees a picture of a given quality level. For example, highly compressed video often does away with astounding amounts of color data, while keeping more luminance (brightness) information to distract the eye from the lack of color saturation by the fact that the picture appears sharp.

The amount of motion, contrast, and even straight edges in your footage can make a significant difference in optimal compression of your video. With MPEG, there are two general rules of thumb you can use. The first one is that, for the most part, more bits per second means better pictures. The second rule is that more bits per second means fewer seconds of video on the disc. As your video gets longer, you need to consider how much space is available on a DVD and reduce bitrate accordingly.

VBR stands for *variable bitrate,* and CBR stands for *constant bitrate.* CBR means that the bitrate of the file is constant and unchanging, but MPEG is not a video codec that has to be restricted to a single bitrate or file size over time. MPEG can expand and contract its data stream based on the needs of the footage, through the use of VBR and two passes over the footage. VBR is typically the way to produce the highest-quality results in the smallest file.

With VBR MPEG, high action (with a lot of motion covering a high percentage of the screen) occupies a lot of data. On the other hand, footage of a person walking on the beach 100 yards away from the camera, with the remaining 98% of the screen space occupied by the sky, will take very little data, because the sky is unchanging. In order to budget those bits, the MPEG encoder must get a peek at the footage before it attempts to compress it. That way, the encoder knows where the data needs will be high and where they will be low. The almost oversimplified explanation is that the encoder then creates a plan, if you will, on how best to compress the video, based on the maximum bitrate you specified, but also with attention to maximizing efficiency where it can. After this first pass to assess the material's requirements, the second pass is the compression pass—hence the *2 Pass* you see beside the VBR choices in the Encoding panel Preset.

So why in the world would you even want CBR, you ask? Well, there's a trade-off for that extra quality you get with VBR: time. It takes much longer to do a VBR compression pass than a CBR, not only because it's actually two passes, but also because it also takes some extra time for the encoder just to do the compression pass alone. If you have a client breathing down your neck for a look at a rough edit of a project and you have to make the overnight courier, chances are that the quality you would gain by using VBR wouldn't be worth missing the plane. However, if you are creating a disc that will be a master for duplication of that project, VBR may very well be worth the extra effort. In the end, you must examine the results and judge for yourself which trade-offs make sense.

Under DVD Burner panel:

1   In the DVD Burner pop-up menu, you will see the available DVD burners on your system.

2   Click on Rescan if the DVD burner does not appear. If it still does not appear, check to make sure you have compatible blank DVD media loaded. (If you connected or powered on a DVD burner after you launched Premiere Pro, it won't be recognized unless you close and relaunch Premiere Pro.)

3   Select the number of copies you wish to burn.

4   The Burner Status will indicate whether or not there is a burner with media detected.

5   You can select whether you want to Record, Test Only, or Test and Record your DVD. (Test simulates recording the DVD to check the blank disc for errors; Test and Record runs a test first and records only after the disc has been verified as having no errors.)

The DVD Burner panel in the Export to DVD dialogue.

You can select the Summary panel to verify your settings. When your settings are complete, click on the Record button to start the process.

The next question in your mind is sure to be, "How long should this take?" Unfortunately, the answer is, "It depends." The speed of your processor, the amount of RAM in your system, the amount of free space on your hard drive, the length of your program, and the speed of your DVD burner will all play a role. If the program is long and you are compressing with VBR, you may have quite a wait. For a 5-minute corporate piece being compressed CBR for a proof copy, you may be able to complete the process fairly quickly. Test your system before you promise results, because the system on which all this is being done is still the biggest variable.

Adobe Media Encoder

If your project will be playing back from a file, whether it's an MPEG-2 file for later authoring to DVD, or an MPEG-1, QuickTime, Windows Media, or Real Media CD-ROM, or Internet-based file, you will need to *transcode* the material to the proper compression format before you can deliver the project. The Adobe Media Encoder is included with Premiere Pro to accomplish that task.

From the pulldown menu, select File ▶ Export ▶ Adobe Media Encoder. The Transcode Settings dialogue will open.

In the Format pop-up menu, choose between MPEG-1 and MPEG-2 presets for DVDs, SVCDs, and VCDs. Or you can choose customizable settings, as well as QuickTime, Windows Media, and Real Media settings.

In the case of MPEG compression for VCD, SVCD, or DVD, it is best to stick with the presets under the pop-up if you are unsure of the settings to use. If you spend some time examining all the options, you will see that the DVD standard requires certain settings to be compatible with the majority of consumer DVD players out there. The MPEG-2 standard is much broader than the DVD standard, and it is possible to create an MPEG-2 stream that won't play back on a DVD player. The presets are a great way to ensure that your work will be properly formatted for the media you choose to distribute your project.

A VCD can be played on some DVD players and on most computers but uses MPEG-1 compression and is burned to a CD-R. I really don't agree with calling anything that is a product of digital output "VHS quality," because we're comparing apples and oranges; however, that is typically how MPEG-1 is characterized. It is much lower in quality than DVD MPEG-2.

An SVCD is a more obscure format that burns a short amount of video onto a CD-R. SVCD uses an MPEG-2 compression scheme that is still a bit lower in quality than DVD video but better than MPEG-1. Some DVD players will play it, but support for it is still a bit spotty.

DVD, as we know, uses MPEG-2 with particular settings.

Each format option will have a number of presets available from the Presets pop-up menu underneath the Format pop-up menu. You can choose the appropriate preset or customize your own setting in the Video and Audio panels in the left-hand Summary column. If you want to save a customized preset, you can use the Save Preset button (which looks like a floppy disk) in the top right of the dialogue, to save the preset for later use. To load a custom preset, select the Load Preset button, which looks like a folder.

The Transcode Settings dialogue for the Adobe Media Encoder.

Exporting Media

There are times when you need to export material from Premiere Pro for processing or use in other programs. Premiere Pro can export a clip, a sequence, or a section of a clip or sequence as a motion clip in a variety of formats. You can also export audio and still frames.

One final note on compression: we are covering the basics of how Premiere Pro interacts with video compression in general. We won't be covering the tiny, or even the many not-so-tiny, details of the implications of the various compression schemes available. There are entire books that struggle to be comprehensive and timely on that topic.

As I mentioned in the DVD section earlier, video compression can seem to be more sorcery than science. In many aspects, the significance is in the subtleties. The compression types available to each user will vary, and their uses will be different, depending on what type of workflow you have.

Exporting a Movie

You can export part or all of a clip or a sequence as a motion clip by selecting File ▶ Export ▶ Movie.

In the Export Movie dialogue, you can browse to the destination for your exported file. To change the attributes of your exported material, click on the Settings button in the bottom right of the window. This will open another dialogue, where you can choose how to set up your file for export.

The Export Movie dialogue. Note the Settings button to access the specific settings panels.

In the General panel:

1 Select the desired option from the File Type pop-up menu (you will be able to use the Compile Settings button to the right for GIF file selections).

2 Select the range. For a timeline export, you will choose between the complete sequence and the Work Area; for a clip export, you will choose between the complete clip or just the in and out points.

3 In the check boxes below, choose whether to export video, audio, or both. You can choose to have Premiere Pro automatically add your exported media to the Project window when you're finished—not to mention whether or not you desire your computer to beep at you when it's done.

4 Embedding Options enables other Adobe programs to associate back to this Premiere Pro project. Select Project when the file you are exporting will be used in another application that has an Edit Original option, such as After Effects and Adobe Encore DVD.

The General panel in the Export Movie Settings dialogue.

The Video panel has these settings:

- The Compressor pop-up indicates the codec Premiere Pro will use to export your file.

- Color Depth may or may not present you with options. This is an important setting when you are exporting for the Web and need to reduce your color depth considerably, or when you want to preserve the alpha channel on your exported clip and require a 32-bit color depth.

- Frame Size will be tied to whether or not your chosen export codec has support for multiple frame sizes. For example, DV will always be 720 × 480 pixels for NTSC and 720 × 576 pixels for PAL.

- Whether or not there are options under Frame Rate also depends on the compressor you've chosen for output.

- Pixel Aspect Ratio will usually be set properly when you set the compression type for your file. If you are unsure, try the default setting first. Changing this option can cause problems with the interpretation of your file by other applications—or even by Premiere Pro.

- The Quality setting, when available, can affect file size. You may want to try this at different levels with some codecs, because a very small adjustment can sometimes create a noticeable difference in quality.

- The Data Rate settings can be used, on compatible compression types, to limit the data rates of exported files. The Recompress check box and its pop-up can be used always to recompress the existing material, or only to compress when needed to fit within the specified data rate.

The Video panel in the Export Movie Settings dialogue.

The following settings are in the Keyframe and Rendering panel:

- Rendering Options adjustments include a field dominance choice, which is similar to where this option appears elsewhere in Premiere Pro. Choices include Upper, Lower, and No Fields (Progressive Scan).

- Click the Deinterlace Video Footage check box to create noninterlaced content from interlaced video material.

- The Optimize Stills check box indicates whether any still frames that are on screen during the clip should be imaged as one frame, held for a given period, or treated as actual video frames, creating 30 (or whatever the frame rate is) new frames every second. Check this box to hold the frame, creating a smaller exported file.

- Keyframe Options will only be available with certain compression types, which use compression over time.

The Keyframe and Rendering panel in the Export Movie Settings dialogue.

Compression keyframes are the frames that are stored as complete pictures, whereas the frames between the keyframes (often called *delta* frames) are stored as amendments to the keyframe, stretching until the next keyframe is loaded as a complete picture, then starting the process again. More frequent compression keyframes can create a higher-quality file; less frequent compression keyframes create a smaller file at a lower quality. Finding the balance between file size and picture quality is the eternal challenge of image compression. Most likely, you will have to experiment to find the right balance.

The Audio panel offers the following settings:

• The Compressor choices available to you will depend on your compression choice in the video panel. Uncompressed audio is obviously the highest quality.

• The Sample Type setting is adjustable up to 32 bits, and the Channels setting specifies whether the file is mono or stereo.

• Interleave controls how much audio is loaded into RAM to be processed with the video. A setting of 1 means that one frame of audio is loaded with each frame of video. Adjust this setting if you are hearing pops or clicks in your audio (a larger number will result in more audio being loaded at once, requiring more RAM for proper playback). Most video cards work well with interleave settings of 1/2- or 1-second audio interleave.

The Audio panel in the Export Movie Settings dialogue.

When your settings are complete, click on OK to accept them, close the Export Movie Settings dialogue, and go back to the Export Movie window. Once you've chosen a location, click Save.

Exporting a Frame

To export a still frame for use in another application, such as Adobe Photoshop, select File ▶ Export ▶ Frame. A dialogue will open so that you can browse to the location where you want to save the file.

You will see the familiar Settings button for specifying file type and compression. The only part of this dialogue that wasn't covered in the Export Movie section is the file types available to export in the General panel.

The available file types are as follows:

- Targa, or .tga file, which supports 16- 24- or 32-bit RGB images.

- TIFF, or .tif file, which can be RGB, CMYK, Lab, or Indexed-Color, is supported by almost all image-editing and paint programs.

- Windows Bitmap, or .bmp file, which supports multiple color depth RGB, Indexed-Color, and Bitmap Color images, is a standard file type for Windows and DOS computer platforms.

The Export Frame Settings dialogue.

- CompuServe GIF, or .gif file, which creates a very small file but is of a lower quality than any of the others. These LZW-compressed images support Indexed-Color images and tend to be ideal as a file for the Internet or an image to be e-mailed to someone for reference purposes.

Often a video or film clip needs some alteration. Perhaps the convenience store sign needs to be removed from the skyline of the gladiator movie, or the wires that are levitating the movie ghost have to be painted out, etc. This process of drawing directly on captured motion frames is called *rotoscoping* and is an essential tool in video, but even more so in feature film production. You can export motion clips as sequential still images for use in Photoshop or some other application:

1   First select File ▶ Export ▶ Movie to open the Export Movie dialogue.

2   Click on Settings.

3   For File Type, choose Windows Bitmap, TIFF, or Targa. (The animated GIF file format creates a motion clip, not individual frame files.)

4   Select whether you want to export the entire project or just the frames that are included under the work area bar from the Range menu.

5   Specify your export options in the Video and Keyframe and Rendering menus.

6   Close the Settings window and return to the Export Movie dialogue. Set the destination for your numbered files. (I recommend creating a new folder to keep all your associated frame files together and organized.)

7   Remove the wires and the convenience store sign...

Name your file with a number as the last part of the file name, indicating how many digits you want in the frame numbers. If your filename is LogoOpen, you might want to type in *LogoOpen000*. The frames will be numbered as LogoOpen 00001, LogoOpen00002, ... LogoOpen00050, etc. All frames in the sequence must have the same number of numerals in the name to be reimported properly.

Note: After you've completed your work on the still images, you can reimport them and create a clip by choosing File ▶ Import and selecting the first sequential frame. Before importing, check the box labeled Numbered Stills at the bottom of the window. The stills will be compiled into a clip in Premiere Pro.

Select the first numbered frame of a still sequence and check the Numbered Stills box at the bottom of the Import dialogue to compile the stills into a clip in Premiere Pro.

Exporting Audio

To export audio for use in another application, such as Adobe Audition, select File ▶ Export ▶ Audio. A dialogue will open so that you can browse to the location where you want to save the file.

The options available in the Settings dialogue are identical to the settings covered in the section on Exporting a Movie.

INTERACTING
WITH OTHER
ADOBE SOFTWARE

As the process of video editing changes and new advances in computer hardware and software continue to make desktop computers more powerful, desktop computers are taking over many roles formerly dominated by expensive dedicated workstations and proprietary or extremely specialized software. Graphics, special effects, audio production, and post-production that used to be done on many different specialized systems—or even by specialized companies—all continue to migrate to inexpensive, off-the-shelf computer systems.

Because computers can accomplish various functions through the use of different software, a small production staff with a few computers can now do all of the jobs previously mentioned—and then some. The laptop computer on which I'm writing this book has software to do everything previously mentioned (now, if I only had all those skills). Although the laptop may not be as fast as my desktop systems, it is far more portable.

Adobe has several software packages that are designed to complement Premiere Pro in meeting the needs of those of us who must complete a variety of tasks, most of the time without leaving the computer we're working on.

Working with Adobe Photoshop

Adobe Photoshop has long been the gold standard for photo and graphic manipulation software. Once used primarily by print layout artists and photographers to retouch or manipulate photographs, Photoshop's value for image manipulation in video post-production has become increasingly apparent in recent years.

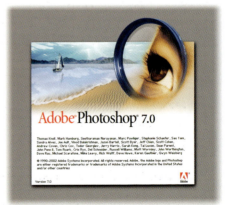

We use Adobe Photoshop to create some sophisticated titling and masks, to work with client logos and graphic content, and, of course, to manipulate still images.

New

Name: Untitled-1

Image Size: 10K

Preset Sizes: Custom

- Custom
- Default Photoshop Size
- Letter
- Legal
- Tabloid

Mode:

- 2 x 3
- 4 x 6
- 5 x 7
- 8 x 10

Contents
- ⊙ White
- ○ Background
- ○ Transparent

- 640 x 480
- 800 x 600
- 1024 x 768
- 468 x 60 web banner

- 720 x 540 Std. NTSC 601
- 720 x 534 Std. NTSC DV/DVD
- 864 x 486 Wide NTSC 601
- 864 x 480 Wide NTSC DV/DVD
- 768 x 576 Std. PAL
- 1024 x 576 Wide PAL
- 1280 x 720 HDTV 720P
- 1920 x 1080 HDTV 1080i

- A4
- A3

- B5
- B4
- B3

OK

Cancel

New document size presets in Adobe Photoshop 7.0.

Import

We'll need a Photoshop file with several layers. In Photoshop 7.0, you can choose the proper document size from the New dialogue. Photoshop 7.0 says that 720 × 534 pixels is the frame size required for NTSC DV/DVD. Although this is the proper image aspect with square pixels, the actual picture size of NTSC DV is 720 × 480 pixels. This is because the pixels in DV are not square, but slightly taller than they are wide. For other NTSC formats or PAL, there are document presets, as well.

(Photoshop CS can create documents with nonsquare pixels.)

What all this means is that the 534-pixel tall document will stretch off the top and bottom of the screen a bit. You may want to practice with Photoshop frame sizes and Premiere Pro, even if you're an experienced Premiere user. Still documents are handled at their actual size in Premiere Pro, rather than attempting to force-scale the image into the video frame size.

1 Create a document in your desired size in Photoshop and create several layers with some content.

2 Save the document.

3 Launch Premiere Pro and go to File ▶ Import.

4 Find your Photoshop file and select it.

At this point, you will get a dialogue asking you to make some choices. The Import Layered File dialogue has a menu option to import your Photoshop file.

You can import Photoshop documents as footage (single layer) or as a sequence.

To load the file as footage will result in all layers being merged and acting like one still image. You won't be able to manipulate any layers separately. If you import as footage, you have the option, toward the bottom of the dialogue, to load all the layers merged together or to load a particular layer. (This is one of those times when naming your Photoshop layers something descriptive really comes in handy.)

You can choose to load individual layers from a Photoshop file. Normally, I name my layers much more descriptively than this—with good reason.

If you choose to load one layer, you can choose between Document Size and Layer Size. Document Size refers to the size of your Photoshop document; the Layer Size option will look at only the area that the content on the layer occupies and will crop it tightly, eliminating empty document space. If you have carefully arranged the layers within the document in Photoshop, choose Document Size, because Layer Size will cause all the layer content to be centered by Premiere Pro, discarding any position information.

On the left is the layer loaded at document size; the text is in the top left corner of the Photoshop document. On the right is the same layer loaded at layer size; the text has been centered in the frame because the text is the only content on the layer.

If you choose to load the file as a sequence (as opposed to footage), all the layers will be loaded separately and assembled in their own sequence, layered on the timeline the way they were laid out in Photoshop. This can be a very productive way to work with Photoshop documents, because you can load the layers and manipulate them in their own sequence. By preproducing your Photoshop file's motion or effects in this way, you can drag the Photoshop sequence from the Project window into your master sequence—with the entire Photoshop document and all the individually handled layers as one easy-to-handle clip.

An easy way to illustrate the benefits of working this way is to consider a multi-element graphic that assembles itself through different components flying in and all landing exactly on their mark to form a finished logo. It's easiest to construct a logo that has several elements in Photoshop, perfecting the relative size and placement of each individual element on each layer. When you import the Photoshop document as a sequence, all the elements are lined up precisely, allowing you to create your motion or effects with an ending home position, as opposed to attempting to line up the components by sight in Premiere Pro.

Export

To export material to Photoshop from Premiere Pro, you have several options. Photoshop will load any of the still document formats that Premiere Pro will export (BMP, TIFF, Targa, or GIF). Photoshop can also load a Filmstrip file, which is available when you export a clip (as opposed to a frame). I usually recommend that users export numbered images, as explained in Chapter 10. Filmstrip files can be awkward to handle, and I find it easier to work on a series of frames loaded into one document and stacked as layers in one Photoshop file. That way, I can see changes lined up between layers instead of scrolling through the frames all laid out on one large canvas.

Working with Adobe After Effects

Adobe After Effects 6.0 has become a favorite tool of many motion graphic artists. This software lets you do very sophisticated layering of multiple video and still images or graphics, create incredibly complex text animations, and basically just accomplish demanding video effects tasks that Premiere Pro really isn't designed to do (or, in some cases, doesn't do as well or as easily).

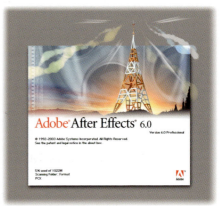

After Effects can create rendered video files to be imported into Premiere Pro in the conventional way that you might import any video clip.

Premiere Pro doesn't load After Effects project files, but it can open the After Effects project file when you select Edit Original on the rendered clip that came from the project. In After Effects, go to Composition ▶ Make Movie to open the Render Queue dialogue. In the render settings for your composition, select the hot text next to Output Module to open the Output Module Settings dialogue. In this dialogue, for Embed select Project Link. Premiere Pro will automatically open the After Effects project where the video file was created.

The Output Module Settings dialogue in After Effects 6.0.

After Effects will also open a Premiere Pro project should you want to work with advanced keying or effects within a Premiere Pro project. In After Effects, go to File ▶ Import and select a Premiere Pro project to import.

Note: This feature is enabled by a plug-in that installs with Premiere Pro. If you have installed After Effects after installing Premiere Pro, you may have to install this plug-in manually or reinstall Premiere Pro to use this feature.

Selecting a Premiere Pro project file to import into After Effects.

The following are some important factors in how Premiere Pro project files in After Effects are handled:

- Clips remain in their folder arrangements. Subfolders will show up correctly, and sequences will convert to After Effects compositions within their proper folders, as well. Photoshop layers and sequences will transfer as if they had been loaded directly into After Effects.

- Cross dissolves will convert to clip opacity changes.

- Motion Fixed Effects properties will translate into After Effects.

- The Crop video filter will convert to an After Effects layer mask.

- Effects using After Effects filters in Premiere Pro will transfer directly, but other filters may not translate properly or work at all.

- You can render Premiere Pro sequences from After Effects to be used in Premiere Pro or as final output of your project.

Working with Adobe Audition

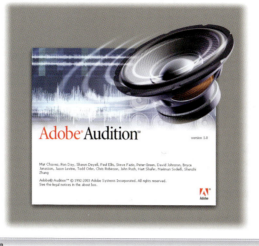

An example of creating audio to video in Adobe Audition.

Audio is often the ignored component in the world of video editing. Although Premiere Pro has some of the best audio tools available on any video editing software package, there will still be times when a dedicated, versatile audio editing and production software package will be needed to enhance or (unfortunately, in some cases) to fix your material.

Adobe Audition is really several tools in one. You can edit audio files and create multitrack audio mixes (up to 128 stereo tracks). You can also use Audition's looping capabilities to create your own music beds, using any of the thousands of music loops included with the software or generally available.

There are different ways to work with Adobe Audition in your workflow. You can produce music and sounds in Audition to be imported into Premiere Pro, or you can take video clips with sound and work on the audio portion of the video clip itself.

When you output an Audition project, you can create your sound file so that the Audition session and mixdown files can be accessed via the Edit Original option in Premiere Pro. Select Options ▶ Settings and click on the Data tab. Select Embed Project Link data for Edit Original functionality.

Embedding a project link in your Audition projects will enable Premiere Pro to link to the project from the sound file in your video project, using Edit Original.

Working with Adobe Encore DVD

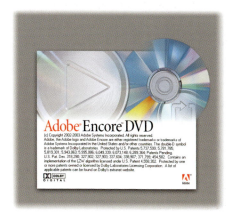

DVDs are becoming a preferred method for distributing video content. And why not? The video quality is superior to most widely available consumer videotape titles, which are usually offered on VHS. The audio quality is superb, and with surround sound available on DVDs...well, let's just say the DVD is most definitely here for a while.

When you distribute your content on DVD, there are a couple of ways to go about it. We described Adobe Premiere Pro's direct Export to DVD earlier, but if you want a truly sophisticated title, you will need to *author* the DVD. Authoring will give you the ability to create menus and make your disc interactive, offering your viewers options.

Adobe Encore DVD is one of the newer kids on this particular block, but it definitely isn't short on features.

Although Encore can be your tool for the authoring process, you will want programs like Adobe Photoshop and After Effects to create your graphics and motion menus, and you will need a program like Premiere Pro to create your finished movie.

A standard video DVD uses MPEG-2 video files. If you are creating a program in Premiere Pro that is intended for authoring in Adobe Encore DVD, you need to export a file from Premiere Pro that is the audio and video of your completed project (see Chapter 10: Exporting Media on page 170). You can either export a clip in the native format in which you are editing, such as DV, and let Encore change the file to MPEG-2 when you burn the disc, or you can output the MPEG-2 file directly from your Premiere Pro timeline (see Chapter 10: Adobe Media Encoder on page 168). I prefer to encode my MPEG-2 files from the timeline to avoid duplicate steps, not to mention that the MPEG-2 file is smaller than a full-resolution master program clip of DV or MPEG video.

Another reason to export MPEG-2 from the timeline in Premiere Pro is that you can create markers on your timeline, and those positions will remain attached to the file. This means you can create chapter points at those marker points almost effortlessly. If you were to export an AVI from Premiere Pro for MPEG-2 encoding in Encore DVD, there would be no way to retain this marker information.

By using the Embed Project option in Premiere Pro's export dialogue, all these programs can link back to a project in Premiere Pro from the exported file using the Edit Original command.

Additional Premiere Pro Resources

First of all, the online help available within the software from the Help pulldown menu is very useful and, of course, always right at hand. I always start there to address my questions.

www.classondemand.net

Class On Demand offers a series of instructional DVDs that are solid information, and the host may seem strangely familiar.

Other resources are available on the Web:

http://www.adobe.com/support/forums/main.html

Adobe's own user forums. You will find a forum for every product in the Adobe lineup here. Maybe Premiere Pro isn't the only one that interests you.

http://www.creativecow.net

A strong community of media production pros and enthusiasts. Adobe Premiere Pro is one of more than 100 forums focusing on various aspects of video, film, audio, and rich media production. (You may recognize a few of the moderators.) The site also includes articles, reviews, and a free newsletter.

http://www.dmnforums.com

Digital Media Net's lineup of user forums includes one that focuses on Premiere Pro. This is a large site with many resources. Although participation in the forums is free, paying a modest membership fee allows access to the site with minimal advertising.

http://www.stevengotz.com/premiere.htm

Steven Gotz maintains one of the best free Premiere Pro resource sites on the Web. Links, tutorials, and FAQs are regularly updated.

http://www.wrigleyvideo.com

Curt Wrigley has built a following for his site with tutorials that range from entry level to imitating effects of major motion pictures. Another free site worth frequenting for a novice or expert Premiere Pro user.

http://www.adobepremiereprohelp.com

The Premiere Pro Help Web site is designed as an online Help companion for Premiere Pro, with an extensive library of screen movie and multimedia tutorials. Scheduled to go online in January of 2004, the site will include discussion forums and a tutorial-on-demand service for a modest subscription fee.

Enjoy.

Tim Kolb

Index